FRESH
Out of Hell

Escaping the Negative Influences of Toxic Parenting

ALYSON KAY

Cold Tree Press

Library of Congress TXV1-112-163

Published by Cold Tree Press
Nashville, Tennessee
www.coldtreepress.com

Printed in the United States of America
ISBN 1-58385-069-4

For my Aunt, my Godmother, my Friend.
The one who believed in me when I
believed in nothing.

Acknowledgements

First of all, I wish to acknowledge God for giving me the grace to receive the insights I needed to understand the truth about my life. Without His intervention and guidance there would've been no hope for me.

Profound love and gratitude to my beloved Aunt for taking her job as my Godmother so seriously. She proved to be an unanticipated yet consistent source of unconditional love, support and understanding through some of my darkest times. I will always treasure her presence in my life.

My gratitude and appreciation to my friend and colleague, Lynne, through whom I found encouragement, enthusiasm and consistent support. Her initial insights helped to provide the direction I needed towards finishing this book and facilitate my emergence as a speaker and a writer.

My thanks to Ginni, the sister I never had, who offered friendship, love, and an empathetic ear throughout my "reparenting" process. It was through Ginni and her family that I most felt the true meaning of family and for this I am profoundly grateful.

My gratitude to my friend and fellow writer, Greg, whose moral support, compassionate commiseration and practical information saw me through the most difficult times of the writing process.

Most sincere thanks to Shirley, the loving midwife and final editor of this work. Her enthusiastic support helped me with the final push to realize its completion.

I acknowledge and thank my friend Gerry for encouraging me to continue writing after I nervously read him the first chapter.

I want to thank and acknowledge my extended spiritual family, though we might not have known who we were at the time; all the clients, colleagues, counselors, strangers and friends who materialized at crucial times in my life to offer support or a kind word, camaraderie, laughter, a place at their holiday table, words of advice, direction or consolation when I needed them the most. Without you I truly would not be here today. I thank and love you all.

Table of Contents

Author's Note

I began writing this book as an "exorcise." Before its writing, I would see my life in sentences of white letters on a black slate every night as I closed my eyes to try to go to sleep. I did not want to think about emotional abuse. I wanted to put it all behind me and move on. But it simply would not let me rest. Apparently something needed to be expressed.

From a practical standpoint, I did not want to give this work the intense focus I knew would be necessary to accomplish its completion. It most certainly would not be fun. I would have to perform a juggling act with the unpleasantness of the past while living with the demands of the present, plus, I am not a good typist. I saw this as a painful, lengthy and daunting task.

However, once I started seeing things in black and white, I began to see the truth of my life, and I, for once, had the clear realization of what I had been through and what I had overcome. I began to feel that this might not be such a wasted effort after all. This was now my opportunity to tell *my* story from *my* perspective and perhaps even help others from the similar circumstances of unconscious parenting and resulting negative consequences through my experiences.

During the course of this revealing and healing process, I've struggled mightily with its every aspect. From daring to write it in the first place and going against the powerful indoctrination of childhood training, to how to present it while still being mindful of the individuals involved.

I've had extreme misgivings about sharing this work. I have moved on in my life and I did not want to go backwards or be punished all over again for past transgressions born of ignorance and sorrow.

I am complimented that most people would never guess my background or what a tremendous struggle its been to get here. They would just see a friend, a neighbor, an employee or fellow club member, just me.

Upon encouragement from close friends and colleagues who have read it, I decided to overcome my fears and embarrassment and share it with others. It is sincerely my hope that should you find something helpful in its pages that you take from it what you need. As its writer and fellow human being I humbly ask for your compassionate understanding. Please note that names have been changed to protect the privacy and dignity of the innocent, the guilty, and those who don't yet know what they are.

I'm not interested in revenge or blame.
My purpose is not to punish or embarrass.
To tell my story, however, I had to tell the truth.
Sometimes the truth hurts...

...But it can also set you free.

Escaping the Negative Influences of Toxic Parenting

ALYSON KAY

PART I: HELL

Chapter 1

A man's foes will be of his own household – Matt. 10:36

From the sidelines I watched as the parade of life passed by. Degrees had been earned, careers blossomed, successes achieved, marriages endured…or not, families created, retirements planned, while I had not even gotten out of the starting gate. Where was I while all this living had been going on?

Well, I had been busy too, but not with the stuff of a normal life. You see, I had been busy unraveling the enormous ball of emotional twine that had choked every aspect of my life. Busy sorting through each and every box and piece of dusty luggage that had cluttered the dark attic of my mind.

But why were my friends free to live their lives, while I was searching for a reason to even be alive? What was so wrong with me? To find out I had to go all the way back to the beginning and that would take time to sort it through…over twenty years.

UNPREDICTABLE AND VOLATILE

Growing up in my family was like living in an emotional minefield. Tinder-dry emotions could explode into a firestorm at any time. A peaceful moment could turn chaotic, contentious and frightening just like that. Most of the time it wasn't clear what triggered the bomb, so you never knew what it was that you should never do again. One had to tread very softly so as not to disturb the sleeping enemy.

My father was a doctor and professor: book-learned, hard-working, emotionally remote, pedantic, inquisitive, explosive, angry, volatile, with a capacity for certain humor, sometimes sadistic.

My mother was an artist: attractive, creative, witty, charming, changeable, manipulative, melancholy, long-suffering, selfish, with a capacity for being mean.

Put these two together and it was pretty much hellish for anyone that had the misfortune to be dependent on them. That would be my two brothers and me.

1

If they were to describe me then, I believe they would agree that their firstborn child and only girl was pathetically timid, reed-thin, unattractive, sickly, fragile, altruistic, not-too-bright, musical, artistic, animal loving and introverted, basically not a child they were proud of. Once, I accidentally walked in on them while they were discussing my apparent lack of intelligence and what to do about it.

The most frightening thing about Mom and Dad was that they could appear so normal. She was so pretty and vivacious, he was a so intelligent, a respected doctor and teacher. By all outward appearances, they were quite a striking couple. The times we did go out as a family, I liked it, because they had to be on their best behavior and it was a pleasant break from the reality of it...

...BUT AT HOME EVERYTHING WOULD CHANGE

My dad was sour and dour most of the time. His scowling looks of obvious displeasure could stop me dead in my tracks. He could always find something to be miserable about, something to complain about, something to have a slamming tantrum about. Everyone and everything outside of himself was wrong, bad or less intelligent. His doom-saying negativity could blast a hole in my delicate balloon of joy and optimism like a 12-gauge shotgun, so I found it wise to keep most things to myself. I shriveled in fear around him and his erratic behavior. Everyone in the household had to defer to his bad moods. Nothing less was tolerated. His philosophy of life was...you're born, you grow up, you marry, you divorce, you get sick, get old then you die. Some of his favorite sayings were "There isn't anything you can't tell me that I don't know;" I've got my beady eyes on you;" "Children should be seen and not heard;" "Carpe Diem, Do it now;" "Spare the rod and spoil the child;" "That, my dear is your problem;" "You don't know what sick is;" and "You monsters"!

Perhaps the most destructive revelation directed at me personally was during one particularly large Thanksgiving Dinner gathering, when, out of the blue, Dad decided to share the fact that I was a "mistake" and a burden to my grandmother who cared for me after I was born, what with all my crying and fussing. This certainly was something I could've lived without ever knowing. My grandmother's jaw dropped at her son's tactless and cruel disclosure and I ran sobbing from the table, convinced now more then ever that I truly did not deserve to be alive.

My mother was a different story. Her feelings of melancholy and frustration with her own life were poured onto me as a small child. She used me as a sort of psychiatric sounding board to vent her feelings rather than get appropriate help for herself or encourage my own emotional development. It was always made clear to me that her feelings were much more important than my own. SHE CAME FIRST. If I ever forgot that and expressed something that I was feeling, there would be hell to pay, in the form of anger, guilt, punitive behavior and the withholding of love, which was intolerable to me. I was her Pavlovian puppy dog, always at her beck and call. That's just the way it was. It would remain that way for years to come.

I never saw any affection between my mother and father. I never saw them hold hands, let alone kiss. Actually, affection of any sort was in short supply at my house. Their immaturity and ineffectual communication skills provided the fodder for some really spectacular arguments that could affect the entire household for months at a time. Dinnertime, during those times, could be particularly unpleasant as they avoided eye contact or speaking to one another directly. Instead, they would pass messages to one another via the children, "John, tell your mother to pass the salt." It was extremely uncomfortable to be placed in the middle of these walls of iciness.

I don't remember a single tender father-daughter moment with my dad. But I do recall feeling somewhat envious when I would see such displays while visiting my classmates' homes. I wanted that affection so much, why didn't I get that from my daddy? It was at these times my belief was reinforced that there must've been something very wrong with me.

The only one who I really felt loving warmth from was my grandfather, who died when I was 8 years old. That was a great loss to me. Not much grieving was displayed and his ashes were unceremoniously placed in a decorative jar under the bathroom sink. Inside, I was despondent at the loss. There was no one to talk to about it.

The truth is that I wasn't stupid, I was just scared most of the time. To say that I was a nervous child would be the understatement of the century. My guts were in a knot each and every minute of each and every day. The histrionics and sudden angry displays always made me feel off-balance and nauseated. If there was a blissful moment of peace, usually ones of my own creation in my room with my paints and pets, it would certainly be short-lived. My serenity was routinely, abruptly and loudly disturbed. I grew to be ever watchful, ever on guard for signs of the next possible outburst. Home was no neutral port in the battles of life…it was the war!

But just like a weary and vigilant soldier in the field, I felt no respite from the specter of the turbulent emotions that lay just beneath the surface. I had to be ever at the ready, ever on guard for the next onslaught. Relief never came.

Needless to say, I was not a happy little girl. I became afraid of absolutely everybody: a checker at the market, the operator on the telephone, the man at the gas station. I believed that under those smiling faces, everyone was like my parents… outwardly pleasant but frightening underneath. If I could've become invisible, I would have gladly done so.

Another source of stress was our teacher at the private school, an overweight, unhappy, heavy-handed misery of a woman, whose great joy in life was to inflict creative and forceful punishment on her young students. Once she picked up my brother, slung him over her bulky shoulder, and placed him outside to stand in the cold, foggy drizzle for hours.

I wasn't as free as my brother. Such an action directed at me would've been unbearable, for many reasons. Although my brother flailed and cursed, he seemed unafraid to take her on. It was at those moments I respected him the most. I wished I could be more like him, defiant and gutsy. But those moments of glory were short-lived because eventually we'd have to go home. When it came to my Father's punishment, my brother wasn't so brave. The verbal abuse, the hand, the belt, the shoe, the board, bamboo sticks all were fair punishment tools utilized on both of us. That's why I chose the quiet, timid approach. I was less apt to be noticed.

The few genuinely joyful moments I do recall came to an abrupt end once I turned eight years old, as I sensed that both parents were not emotionally there anymore. I was on my own. It was then that I understood that I would h ave to endure this emotional pressure cooker for a very long time, so I resigned myself to doing whatever personality contortions I sensed necessary to survive. I actually remember the moment I thought, "Don't ever let them see the real you or you will die." So I made a deal with myself to get out of their way as best as I could.

I did not do well in school; it was hard to study and concentrate. Although I worked very hard to complete the assignments (only because I was afraid of the consequences if I didn't) it was a constant struggle. With the ever-present turmoil, criticism and negativity in the household and at school, I felt ignorant and tongue-tied. It definitely was not a place to thrive and blossom. One time the verbal abuse became so intolerable my brother and I agreed to both jump out of my father's moving car just to get away from it!

My parents separated in my 17th year and chose to make an embarrassing scene at my high school graduation ceremony. This was just the beginning of their mean-spirited, lengthy divorce process. They punished each other and punished me by using me as a "dumping ground" for their problems and to vent just how horrible the other one was. What they d i dn't seem to understand was that if Mom was a "bitch" and Dad was a "bastard", what did that make me? The emotional aftermath inflicted on me by this juvenile, immature and cruel approach to their problems would prove to be extremely detrimental to me and my future relationships for many years to come.

The truth was that I wanted my father's approval and my mother's love desperately. Because I was taught never to talk back or disrespect my parents, it never occurred to me that I had any other choice than to be there for them and be forced to listen to all their vitriolic bile. It twisted me up inside. I didn't want to know this stuff, but I felt trapped with no way out. It was beaten into me to never to talk back. But if I could, I would've said, *YOU ARE BOTH ADULTS, WORK THIS OUT AMONG YOURSELVES, LEAVE THE INNOCENT CHILDREN OUT OF IT!! LEAVE ME OUT OF IT, YOU ARE HURTING ME!!! I DON'T WANT TO KNOW THIS. IT'S NOT MY BUSINESS AND THERE'S NOTHING I CAN DO ABOUT IT ANYWAY.*

But I was afraid of them and the punishments they could inflict and the love they could withhold, so I dared not even allow myself to think this.

During the divorce both wanted me to testify against the other in court. There was no way that I could do this. It made me physically ill to even think about it and I begged not to be asked to do this. They appointed a psychiatrist to find out what was wrong with me and to encourage me to testify. I "flipped out" on purpose. I didn't care if they thought I was crazy, there was no way I could sit there and choose sides as my parents watched me in the courtroom. I would've rather died.

There was no place for me after the divorce. I was now 18. I was to move out into a place of my own and dad was ordered to pay child support until I was 21, something he bitterly resented. My two younger brothers went to live with my mother and I, with no foundation other than the chaos I had experienced all my life, was now expected to be a productive, functioning member of society. But I wasn't.

At 18, in my own apartment, I had no clue as to what was expected of me. Mostly I was needy because I didn't want to be alone. It didn't take long for my "friends" to realize my situation and take advantage of the fact that I was too afraid to tell them to leave. It was at this time that I started to acquire the addictions that would take years of struggle to overcome. I learned to drink whiskey, I learned to smoke, I learned about drugs, I learned about sex. In truth, I was not ready to be on my own. I didn't have the tools to survive. When I was sent out into the world, my parents didn't even pack me a toothbrush. I didn't stand a chance.

On my 21st birthday I received a letter from my dad notifying me that he was now finally and officially through with me. He was bitter that he had to pay child support for the three years. He basically told me that even if I desperately needed help, I should never expect it from him, that if I ended up in the gutter I was not to come to him for help. I had been written off.

That piece of paper crushed my heart and spirit so thoroughly that I could not eat for weeks. I believe I simply gave up the will to live. If not for my brother's attempts to snap me out of it, I believe I would've succeeded.

At 21, I was a self-hating, miserable, sad, hurt, self-destructive, unprepared, emotional cripple who looked for love and comfort anywhere I could find it. I was an enigma, wrapped in a riddle, tied in a knot and left for dead.

So this was their legacy to me. Like my Father would say, "That, my dear, is your problem." It really was my problem...

...SO WHAT DO I DO NOW?

My promise to myself of "Don't ever let them see the real you or you will die" probably kept my spirit from being totally crushed. But the years of emotional bombardment had done their damage. At the point where I was at last on my own, this is what I was left with:

Extreme self hatred - did not feel like I deserved to be alive
No desire to live past 25
Excessive alcohol consumption, smoking, drug experimentation
Distrusted most people, men especially
Feelings of hopelessness, despair
A detached promiscuity
Disdain of tender emotions
Inability to say "No" for fear that people would not like me
Immodest clothing as a tool to attract loving attention
A desperate need for my father's approval
Complete lack of direction or goals
Extreme fear of the future
Preoccupation with doom, disaster and illness
Inability to receive, love, gifts, compliments
Little desire to eat or take care of myself
Purposely putting myself in harm's way and taking dangerous chances
Inability to read people – no intuitive compass
Incessant inner dialogue of negativity about myself and life
Dislike and distrust of God
Running away from problems, emotional situations
Fear of being alone – utter loneliness
Extreme gratitude for ordinary kindness

This was my legacy.

Without knowing any other way, without having examples of loving behavior in my life, I had absolutely no guide, no clue as to how to proceed, what I should do, or even what was wrong. I struggled with the enormous weight of this baggage and its inevitable sad consequences all throughout my early adulthood.

If you've ever wondered what happens to a person brought up in an environment where love and support are real thin, your worst imaginings couldn't come close to the awful reality of it.

Chapter 2

Broad is the way that leads to destruction – Matt. 7:13

HOW EMOTIONAL DEPRIVATION MANIFESTED IN MY WASTED LIFE

*A*lthough some thought I was attractive, I felt ugly, inferior and stupid inside. But, I reasoned, if the only thing I had was my looks, I should play up that part of myself to get what I needed. I'd dress in revealing outfits to attract men but once I had them, I'd club them with a coldness typically reserved for a male "player" after the date. "Yeah, that was great, sure baby, I'll give you a call." The truth was that I figured out pretty early what men really wanted from me, and it wasn't my brains. So I thought I'd turn the tables and do unto them before they did unto me. I went through the motions, but there was no feeling about it. I could cut off my feelings with the swiftness and precision of a surgeon. No love, no tenderness, no pain, no regrets. "See ya!" Nobody would ever get to me. "They might have my body but they would never get my soul" was what I'd be thinking during sex. If there were any decent, loving individuals who truly cared for me among the riff-raff, I doubt if I could've recognized them, let alone do anything about it. So I dismissed the notion of love as irrelevant and inconvenient.

I found eating repulsive, a waste of time, money and energy. A can of chili and a piece of toast every other day was okay by me.

Smoking Kool's took care of the desire for food most of the time. I got up to two packs a day. Having more than a few whiskey sours or tequila shots and going to a dance club was good for losing a few pounds. A fifth of Jack Daniels could be counted on to get the job done when extra "medication" was necessary.

Various drugs helped to lighten the constant depression and alleviate, if only for a moment, the subliminal unease. But getting my "prescriptions" filled introduced me to unsavory people and dangerous situations. Fads like experimenting with hallucinogenics exaggerated my already troubled perceptions. I did not do well with these.

I was sick much of the time, recurrent respiratory illnesses like strep throat and bronchitis were commonplace. Because of my poor care for myself, these ailments would sometimes last for months and produce such congestion that my hearing would become critically impaired. Once I had laryngitis for six months with the resulting rasp lasting for more than five years! While painful, my illnesses afforded me one thing – a legitimate reason to see my dad, who was a doctor. Then there were the "biggies," frequent female trouble, unwanted pregnancy, appendicitis, which healed poorly due to my impatience to allow proper healing, and poorly done oral surgery which nearly caused my death, at 25, incidentally.

Being so desperate for love and friendship, I thought it was a good idea to take orders and shoplift those ordered items for my friends. Of course I eventually got caught, almost ending up in a woman's prison despite my youth.

I was oblivious to danger and didn't take steps to protect myself. I rarely locked my doors. This lack of vigilance facilitated easy access for an intruder who took me from my home at knifepoint as my brother partied with his friends upstairs. I thwarted his attempt to rape me or worse, by screaming and wrenching myself away from him. I was lucky to get away with only deep lacerations to my hands and neck.

Potentially dangerous situations didn't faze me either – Jumping off bridges into murky water, sneaking into five story buildings via the fire ladder, trespassing in dangerous off-limit areas, hang-gliding off the side of a cliff, filming whales in a rubber dinghy, sailing across the ocean with strangers, going on road trips alone. Yes, I was adventuresome to a degree, but these were all designed to impress my dad. I never felt that he liked that I was a girl, so these more masculine endeavors were all for him to take notice and be proud of my toughness.

I was not the best judge of character, as I really didn't feel qualified to judge anyone. After all, who the hell was I? Many "friends" were equally as self-destructive and rudderless as I was. I once found my roommate in my bed with my boyfriend, which I took in stride as I instantly emotionally shut myself off to them both. No explaining, no pleading, no apologies, they were just dead to me. She also thought it was a good idea to invite hard-core drug addicts into our apartment to allow them to shoot up in the bathroom and beg for her rent money to buy more drugs. On more than one occasion, I found that our apartment had been burglarized of our rent money.

Having no direction or goals made a choice of career impossible. I was always naturally artistic, creative and musical, but expression in these areas was strongly diminished or discouraged, making further training in such "frivolous" areas unthinkable. If I did express an interest in these things, "You'll never make a living at it," was what I was summarily told. But what do I do if this is who I am?

My father envisioned me as a clerk typist, nurse or stewardess. I hated typing, the smell of hospitals made me sick, and I didn't want to cut my hair. My mother thought I should be an actress. I was pathetically shy, had a poor self-image and was frightened to death of public speaking. Neither of them knew me too well it seems.

THIS IS WHAT I ACTUALLY DID

- Worked in my boyfriend's parents' restaurant as a waitress for 3 weeks.
- Worked for (who everyone thought was) a reputable photographer next door as a typist, later getting training as a script supervisor for what turned out to be, cheesy low budget porno films he filmed in secret. Was teased and shocked by other crew members for being a virgin and was overtly propositioned by a lesbian.
- Worked as an artist's model, fully clothed, and was nearly raped by one of the stronger male artists who had later invited me on a date. That could've easily been my "first time."
- Worked as secretary for an inventor until he made a pass at me when we were supposed to be going on a sales call. I found myself running to get away from him at night in a bad part of a strange city miles from home
- Considered becoming a police woman or joining the Air Force but was strongly cautioned that it was just a lesbian enclave and I could expect harassment.
- Worked as an apartment manager in one of my mother's buildings; cleaning, painting, wallpapering and rent collecting until threatened with great bodily harm or worse for being the only Caucasian in the building.
- Discovered the Marina. Invented my way into a job at a yacht

brokerage as a decorator and eventually started my own yacht maintenance business with crew and customers. Worked hard, took it seriously, began to learn about responsibilities to others and the rewards of hard work, while being propositioned by an astonishing array of men, young and old.

- Worked at a major film studio in hopes of becoming a film editor. Had clashes with my misogynistic boss who did not believe a woman should be in that business. I left after he was admonished for his behavior and had become angry with me.
- Worked as an assistant to a graphic artist boyfriend, taught myself the basics of graphics and started designing logos for friends for free.
- GOT MARRIED TO AN ALCOHOLIC AFTER KNOWING HIM LESS THAN 3 MONTHS AND MOVED OUT OF TOWN TO LIVE WITH HIM.
- Watched the boat business I worked so hard to build vaporize through mismanagement and carelessness in a few short months after leaving it to my younger brother and mother after my marriage.
- Started at the bottom again, typing cassette labels at a radio station for minimum wage, learned how to write copy and eventually did voice-overs for radio commercials safely hiding behind characters I created.
- Did several TV commercials until my husband became jealous because he'd been in the business 14 years versus my six months and forced me to quit.
- Worked for several ad agencies in various capacities until one of my bosses came under investigation for sexual harassment. He was demoted to a position beneath me and I was given his job after only being there one month. It was intolerable, I had to leave.
- DIVORCED MY HUSBAND AFTER HE SHOT HIS 357 MAGNUM THROUGH THE CEILING OF OUR APARTMENT AND ATTEMPTED TO BULLDOZE OVER THE NEW CARS IN THE NEXT DOOR CAR DEALERSHIP AFTER A DRINKING BINGE.
- Lost 20 pounds and was now an emaciated 104 lbs. at 5'8"
- Lost my job, the radio station didn't want a conflict. We both worked there, but my ex-husband had seniority.
- Had polyps in my throat and was told by my doctor that I had possibly developed throat cancer.
- Discovered freebasing cocaine with my ex-husband who had now become my "friend."

- Moved in with two roommates and was burglarized within the first month.
- Became so emotionally unstable after finding out that my father offered to help my ex-husband to cope with our divorce, that I broke into uncontrollable tears at a job interview. Needless to say I never got the call back.
- Had such a poverty consciousness that I wondered how I'd ever afford to buy shampoo or gasoline when they ran out.
- From grief and loneliness allowed myself to get involved with someone who eventually became a stalker.

I gave up, left town under the cover of darkness and moved back home to MOTHER…

…THEN I FOUND OUT WHAT HELL WAS REALLY LIKE

I was now 30 years old! For all my "creativity," I had accomplished nothing. I was a physical, mental, emotional and financial wreck – No prospects, no job, no friends, no hope. I was fractured and sick down to my very soul. I was a loser and a failure. My life was the pitiful end result of all the horrible things I was taught to believe about myself and about everything around me. I was now reduced to living in a dark, lonely room addition at my mother's house. I never wanted to come out. I wanted to die. But I didn't die. Instead I was given the opportunity to learn the truth whether I wanted to or not.

THINGS HAD TO GET WORSE BEFORE THEY GOT BETTER

Giving up and living at my mother's house after being on my own started to give me the perspective I had been lacking. All this time I thought my problem was just with my dad. But my eyes were being opened, and I didn't like what I saw. Mother was no "innocent," as I had always wanted to believe. I also discovered something else, guilt-inducing and horrifying to me. I DID NOT LIKE THIS WOMAN. There was something very wrong with her: she was changeable; she could be cruel; excessively punitive, and withdraw love at the drop of a hat. She was always miserable and blaming everyone for her miserable life, except when she was drinking. Then it got even worse. She made me uncomfortable and upset all the time, just like when I was a child. But this was my mother! How could I not like my mother? You're supposed to love your mother, buy her warm fuzzy cards for Mother's Day! I did all those things. Of course I loved my mother! Really I did! I lived my life for my mother, there wasn't anything I wouldn't do for her...to shut her up...to get her love...to keep her calm. The awful truth was...I hated her. But there was that commandment about honoring. How do you honor it if you don't like it? How do you honor a liar, alcoholic, and schizophrenic? How do you live with the guilt? Well, I just wouldn't, I'd act like I loved her, even if it killed me, because now I was trapped and I had to live with her. I didn't want to know or admit this to myself; it was too horrible to fathom, so I buried it. This hell grinded on for six months, until there was a reprieve.

Thankfully, one of my mother's renters moved out, which allowed me to move into a separate residence away from her. Now I could concentrate on the things that mattered.

PART 2: PURGATORY

Chapter 3

Be transformed by the renewing of your mind – Rom. 12:2

WE START AGAIN

The house my mother moved me into was an "icebox" almost all year around. The roof on the master bedroom was designed so poorly that rainwater would collect there at depths of up to three feet and remain there for days until it slowly drained. It was a miracle that it didn't collapse on me during a downpour.

The runoff went down through the walls so that they always felt cold and wet. In the wintertime it was excruciatingly cold, as the water trapped in the walls would then freeze. When the weather warmed up, the walls then became a breeding ground for mold and mildew. Who ever said hell had to be hot? But this for now was to be home, and I was grateful for the change of scene.

Truthfully, it could've been a mud hut. I was just extremely relieved to be away from mother because I could better manage the undercurrent of mistrust and disgust from a distance and I could hide my unpleasant feelings more easily.

A few months into this new arrangement, perhaps sensing my increased relief as a threat to unravelling our enmeshed relationship, mother decided to announce a big decision she had made about my future. Out of the blue she surprised me with the fact that she wanted the "icebox" to be my future nest egg. She explained that her mother had done this for her with various properties and now she wanted to do this for me. Although I feigned happiness and gratitude at this news, because I knew that's what she expected me to do, in truth I did not want the icebox house. I thought it was too much. I didn't like it and I found myself immediately dreaming of converting it into a small, manageable, cozy condo as soon as possible. I knew better then to share that dream though. I didn't know why she felt she had to do this but I had suspicions that it was a way to keep control over me even from a comfortable distance. Nevertheless, for the time being, this was to be my home and I would have to make the best of it, because I was beginning to realize that I had some real work to do.

By now I was experiencing the stirrings of change beginning to manifest within me. I was becoming very uncomfortable with the status quo. Handling things as I had before didn't give me what I was looking f o r. I wanted to find another way to live. A sense of peace is what I wanted, what I needed more than anything, and I made up my mind that I was going to have it…at any cost, mother or no mother, house or no house.

FACING FEARS

There were times that my fear of life was so overwhelming I was literally immobilized. Sometimes all I could do was pace the floor and worry myself sick. There were times I was too afraid to leave the house. I was preoccupied with disaster, illnesses, world destruction and poverty. My mind was in an endless swirl of negative and frightening images over which I had no control. No matter how I tried, I couldn't seem to stop the fear.

Everything and everyone frightened me. God frightened me. I believed that I could expect punishment and that I could be struck down at any moment with some debilitating disease or some horrible accident. Nowhere in the world seemed safe or peaceful to me. And it never would, because I carried all this with me wherever I went. With the kinds of things that were in my head, it's no wonder I didn't want to live past 25, no wonder I looked for solace anywhere I could find it.

Hiding and being small served its purpose to get me through my childhood but did not work with actually trying to have a life. Having so many fears severely restricted me on every level. I literally had to start from scratch as a human being. With all the negativity that was pumped into me and without any intuitive compass, I was destined to a very small, narrow, lonely existence if I did not choose to change things.

Because I did not like pain of any kind, I did anything to avoid facing my fears, for that would cause even more pain. Outwardly I could appear competent in limited areas, but with the kind of baggage I had, there were major gaps in my basic education. I constantly worried that people would figure this out about me. Things that others took for granted and learned as a matter of course as they were growing up were things about which I had no clue.

These were seemingly simple things, but they were not simple to me then. They were: feeling loved, feeling safe, trusting people, trusting myself, asking for help, knowing what to do, handling money, talking to people, learning something new, going someplace new, being critiqued, saying no, loving someone, change of any kind. I had a lot to learn and a lot to overcome.

MAKING SENSE OF RELIGION

I wasn't a monk on a mountain; I was a big city girl trying to make her way in this world alone. There was life to face, fears and addictions to overcome, business to handle, relationships to understand. I needed something pertinent and relevant to my experience to help me in a practical day-to-day way to get through this mess. I tried many religions to find where I belonged. All together I was baptized three times in search for the one for me. Most services I attended left me feeling empty and scared of Armageddon. So many nights I had terrifying nightmares and anxiety about being punished in hell for being sinful. I was already in hell, why did I need more of that?

I didn't feel connected to the foreign orthodox religion I grew up with and religion as it was presented simply was not comforting to me. I tried to read the Bible twice, but its archaic language and references didn't make much sense to me. Somehow, though, I couldn't totally discount it; after all, what if there actually was something helpful in there that I could use? How could I tap into it?

Before moving back in with mother, while still living with my roommates, I had consciously started a process to try to improve my life. Although I instinctively knew that I needed to do something to change things, I didn't know how or where to begin. By chance, I picked up a book that had been gathering dust on my shelf for nearly five years, *The Dynamic Laws of Prosperity* by Catherine Ponder. The title intrigued me and I actually began to read it. Ironically this book had been given to me by my mother during one of her many aggressive, self-help promotional campaigns. Though so often I pretended to give an ear, I eventually had come to automatically discount her self-righteous solicitations as irrelevant as she never followed any of their suggestions herself.

But now because my financial situation was so dire, this book held an appeal for me and I actually began to read it. I decided to do every exercise in the book, faithfully. I had nothing to lose. I needed to discover a new way of doing things.

FIRST I HAD TO CHANGE MY MIND

One of the first exercises in Ponder's book was to create a Wheel of Fortune, a kind of Wish Board. It seemed silly but I thought I'd give it a shot.

I allowed myself to fantasize about the kind of life I really wanted. I suspended my own miserable reality and started to let my imagination run free. I looked through all my magazines and newspapers until I found something that caught my attention. I cut out those pictures and pasted them on my Wish Board. I studied it first thing in the morning and the last thing at night.

FOR THE HIGHER POWER
I placed a picture I had of a friendly looking Jesus –
The reality: I was afraid that all the bad things I'd done had made God mad at me.

FOR MYSELF
I pictured a smiling, healthy woman holding fresh vegetables, another one in great shape doing an exercise–
The reality: I was addicted to cigarettes and drank too much, I didn't know how to take care of myself and had bad skin.

FOR WHERE I LIVED
I pictured a house with a backyard, a hammock and a cat–
The reality: I had a small room and shared a residence with 2 strangers.

FOR CAREER
I pictured a smartly dressed, smiling woman in a meeting, shaking hands with a smiling man who was handing her a contract–
The reality: I had no job.

FOR LOVE
I pictured a couple laughing together
The reality: Already once divorced, I now had a frightening stalker to contend with.

FOR TRANSPORTATION

I pictured a beautiful, sleek red sports car –
The reality: I owned a high mileage used car.

FOR CLOTHING

I pictured a gorgeous woman wearing beautiful and colorful clothes–
The reality: I could wear my robe as I rarely went out.

I found that visualizing the kind of life that I wanted was liberating me from the dreary reality of my life and releasing me from my fears. It was fun to free my mind to what seemed to be the impossible. It gave me a sense of hope that it was possible. Plus, I really wanted it to be real.

In addition to the Wish Board, I wrote out daily affirmations and made my own tapes of positive messages about myself and about the world. These affirmations were the complete and total opposite of what was really going on in my mind, the complete and total opposite of how I really felt about myself. It was shocking at first for me to hear such positive things associated with myself. But I was very determined to change the "negative tapes" I'd been programmed with, so I'd listen to them every night before I went to sleep.

Little did I realize that this simple and enjoyable exercise would prove to be the catalyst to changing my whole life.

DEALING WITH THE MENTAL CHATTER

From morning until night, even in my sleep, ceaseless negative chatter pervaded my mind. I tried my best to manage it, but deep inside I thought I was crazy.

Things like "You're so stupid," "What makes you think you can do that?" "Don't be ridiculous, you're a loser," "You'll never make it," "Who do you think you are?" "You'll die in poverty," "You're ugly." And on and on and on. It was hard to function with all this going on all the time. I had to stop the chatter. It was now my number one priority, my main job in life. Either that or I'd have no life.

Each and every negative thought that would present itself had to be dealt with on its own terms…immediately.

If a thought would come in with "You're a poor loser"…

I'd right away counter with *"I am a rich child of a loving Father;*
"You are a mistake, and should've never been born"…

There are no mistakes, I am a divine idea in the mind of God;

"You are poor, and will never amount to anything"…

I am a magnet to my good which is even now on its way to me;

"You're an insecure mess"…

I am harmonious, poised and magnetic;

"You're stupid"…

The genius within me is now released and I fulfill my destiny;

"Look at all the mistakes you've made"…

I am forgiven and governed by God's love alone;

"The world is bad and scary, you will die"…

Divine love now goes before me making easy, successful and delightful my way;

"You'll never amount to anything"…

The Divine Plan of my life now manifests in definite, concrete experiences leading to my heart's desire.

Monitoring my thoughts became my full time job and I took it seriously. My life depended on it. With help from the writings of Ms. Ponder and Florence Shinn's, *The Game of Life and How To Play It*, I became an affirmation-generating machine. By verbalizing, writing, and making audiotapes, all avenues were flooded with positive counter-attacks. No negative thought got past my sentries at the gate, now on full alert. If one had the nerve to appear, it would be caught and shot down right away.

Eventually these positive messages started to take over my way of thinking…about everything! Instead of thinking that I was a fearful, pitiful loser, I started thinking of myself "as a rich child of a loving Father," automatically.

As I started flooding my mind with positivity, changes in my life began to happen. What I was beginning to realize was that the life I had been living, the life I had been programmed to live, was completely off-track with the life I really wanted. I was now making the major adjustments that needed to be made.

REMEMBERING A LIGHT ON MY PATH

After my separation from my first husband, I met a man at an after-work hangout with a group of my peers. Tom was a singer and entertainer there. He was like nobody I had ever met before. He didn't smoke, drink or do drugs and yet he seemed to be genuinely happy. He was a vegetarian and he meditated and wrote affirmations everyday. He was an alien to me. Everybody I knew was into self-abuse of some kind or another, it was just the thing to do. He intrigued me because I couldn't understand how he could live in this world and be so "clean." To this day, I don't know why he liked me. I was full of addictions, anger and misery.

But he was understanding and seemed okay with all of it. As our relationship progressed, he'd share his beliefs and affirmations with me while I would stick my head out the window for a smoke. I learned one thing. He was way, way beyond me and I could never hope to get even a little close to where he was. I really hated him for being so good, because it showed me that it could be done and that you could be happy without "medication." I was angry with him because I realized just how much work I would have to do just to think about getting there. At that point, I didn't believe I could do it.

Our relationship ended when I decided to give my first marriage one last try. I never forgot Tom. His influence over my life was actually very profound for the short time we spent together. He was a light on my pathway that showed me wholeness could be achieved. All I could do was to tuck that possibility away in my mind for future use.

LEARNING TO TRUST GOD

As bad as my life had been, at least it was predictable. Trusting God and the Universe was going to take me into the unknown and that was extremely frightening to me. I didn't like change in the first place and I certainly didn't want to do the work required of me to change my life. I wanted it to change for the better all by itself. I had been counting on it. But of course changes never came and things never got better.

Then there was the other side of it. What would people think of me? If I trusted a higher power would I become some kind of a freaky religious pod person? How would I fit in to society? At least my bad habits got me some camaraderie; in fact, I always had lots of company when I wanted to self-destruct. The church people I had come in contact with were fearful and disdainful of others not of their beliefs. I did not feel I could go to them for any kind of real help without experiencing some ulterior motive on their part.

But to me, trusting God was like jumping off a cliff. Would anybody catch me? Or would I land with a thud in an unknown place that was worse than where I was already? Would I be punished for every bad thing I had done? Or would there be mercy? I was really scared. But, as scary as choosing to trust God was, I reasoned that it couldn't be worse than the mess I had brought about on my own. After struggling with myself for quite a while, I decided to let myself fall.

To my surprise, instead of the hard landing I had feared, it felt like I was being carried and gently placed into a new and peaceful land filled with guidance, love and protection for my every step.

God, to me, turned out not to be an imperious, punitive, remote old man like my dad, but a loving, benevolent energy that was and always had been guiding me to my highest good.

STEPPING OFF THE MERRY-GO-ROUND

There were times when living hurt so bad it was hard to even breathe. The pain of so many losses – death, divorces, health and financial problems, and the eventual realizations and insights into undeniable truths about myself and my family – sometimes left me in an emotional fetal position in the corner of life. It was not hard for me to be isolated and alone for weeks at a time trying to cope with the grief, physical pain and depression resulting from these challenges, betrayals, heart-breaks and emotional "bubble-ups."

At first, during those times of stress and challenge, I did what many people do to get through…I drank to numb myself and escape. But I had so many of these painful times that had I continued with this self-destructive method of coping, there would've been nothing left of me when and if it was ever going to be over. I would've ended up dissipated and destroyed. Plus, drinking added yet another problem to my arsenal of problems…addiction. Actually, there wasn't enough alcohol in the world to cure what was ailing me. All it did was compound it and make things worse. Many times I would end up so sick from over-consumption that it would take days to recover from my self-poisoning. It also added to my mental and physical distress, making things appear even more hopeless then ever.

Another source of my confusion at this time was the impression that everybody handled things this way. The avoidance of dealing with one's sorrows had almost become the national pastime. A good time at all costs and the avoidance of pain of any kind seemed to be the things to strive for; that's what mass quantities of food, alcohol, money, drugs, sex, shopping, games, entertainment and gossip were for. It seemed that the acquisition of money, power and status were drummed into us as desirable above all else. It had become clear to me that people were not comfortable with pain, theirs or anybody else's; better to just stifle it, avoid it or tranquilize it, bury it and move on. Now, here I was, daring to go against the grain to look at the specter of a source of my pain and heal it if I could.

Feeling like I did was embarrassing. What would people think? It would be obvious that I had no control over my life or myself. It would be obvious that I hadn't been successful on any level. I wanted to die of shame. I wanted to conceal it and pretend it was all right. I reasoned that I could try to fake it. But the truth was, I couldn't any more.

What I tried so hard to bury and manage could no longer be managed. I had to learn how to live the reality of my life, such as it was, despite what people might think about me. I had to let go of what society's concept of success was. Success to me had become perhaps getting through the next five minutes without a drink or a smoke.

Once I realized that I had to unhook from the herd mentality and find my own way, I made a promise to myself that I would do whatever was necessary to make it, no matter what any one thought of me. My life depended on it. I would have to do it on my own because there was no earthly support team behind me, no family, no therapist, no best friend to urge me on and offer me comfort. I had to get the courage to do it alone or die waiting for help that might never come.

It was time to clean up my act.

Chapter 4

You shall have no gods before me – Deut. 5:7

OVERCOMING MY ADDICTIONS

*I*n the 1970's, drug use and experimentation was so prevalent that it just seemed like a rite of passage. Everybody did it. In my group, I was actually one of the last holdouts, which made me even more of a prime target for "conversion." My friends at the time knew I couldn't stand marijuana. But one day a boyfriend came over with something "extra special" just for me. Whatever it was, made me feel disembodied and lethargic and it was difficult to speak or walk. "Something special" turned out to be angel dust, a dangerous animal tranquilizer. At first it really scared me and I was angry with him for giving it to me, but eventually I came to appreciate its numbing effect and the momentary peace it gave me. I found that if I could regulate its dose, I could create a pleasant "tropical vacation" kind of feeling without the other harsh and frightening effects. I liked that I thought I could control it. Of course I really couldn't. A few times the stuff was so potent I couldn't control any aspect of my experience and I had what might be characterized as a "bad trip," but that was the chance I was willing to take. Pills were also good for altering my mood. After my problematic appendectomy I was prescribed Placidyls, an extremely strong sedative, which I came to rely upon quite heavily.

Later on, cocaine became the big thing. Once I experienced the initial euphoria I tried to recreate it every time thereafter. It had that wonderful numbing effect I needed. Honestly, I just wanted to alter my consciousness any way that I could because I really couldn't stand to be in my own skin. I didn't care how or what got me there. Fortunately for me I did not have a lot of money, so my usage was restricted by my budget.

Alcohol was definitely the more accepted way to go. After work, when I had work, I could go for happy hours with peers, if something good happened, I could celebrate with drinks, if I got dumped, I could drown my sorrows, if I wanted to loosen up, dance and meet people I could go to clubs and drink. And, if I wanted to dull emotional pain of any kind, good old alcohol was readily available, relatively cheap and it was legal. At first, drinking seemed to be the ticket. It was fun, it was liberating. I didn't have to be me when I was drinking. But there was always the morning after. In my case many mornings after, when I would promise myself…no more.

It seemed I could go for a while without alcohol, but it was everywhere, and I found it hard to resist. Plus, when something shook me up or got me fearful or anxious, which was a lot, that's the first thing I'd reach for. Then too, if I were drinking I'd have to smoke. They went hand in hand. At my peak I was up to two packs a day. Of course by then, they were at least low tar.

I don't think I was ever really comfortable with the damage I was inflicting on myself with my addictions. I felt guilty because I really knew better. But I couldn't live with the pain that I had been working so hard to cover up. I wanted relief from its incessant presence, so I used the smoking, drinking and drugs to hide from it. Of course, these things didn't make me actually feel better. Many days I felt absolutely terrible. But I didn't care, because for a few precious moments I felt free.

Because of the guilt and my financial situation, drugs were the easiest to give up. One day I really saw myself in the mirror after a night of cocaine. I felt ashamed. A little voice inside me asked, "What are you doing?" My pitiful response was "destroying myself." I stopped that very day and never touched it again.

COURAGE TO QUIT

I instinctively knew that quitting smoking would be the most difficult for me because I had been using it as an emotional cork for nearly 12 years. I was afraid of what I would unleash if I ever did have the guts to quit. That scared me, to be that out of control really scared me.

I finally got up my courage to quit when I heard about a place called Physician's Clinic. It was discovered that if you shot a certain anesthetic into someone's neck and earlobes, 90% of patients lost the desire for nicotine long enough to get them through the critical first few days. This sounded serious. I hated shots. It sounded like it was something that would work for me, because it meant that I, too, was serious. The clinicians explained that I needed to get a ride to the clinic, because I would not be able to drive after the shots were administered.

Prior to this I had tried going cold turkey, the Schick Center, a rubber band on the wrist or chewing gum. Nicotine patches and gum were unavailable then. I found that I'd be successful for a time but ultimately found it unbearable to continue.

My mother and brothers had been on my back to quit for years. So now that I was building up the courage to do just that, I asked for their help to get me to the clinic about 20 miles away when the time would come the following week. They promised they would help me.

The morning of the big day came. I anxiously called my mother for the ride and for her promised support to get me through this big challenge. Much to my surprise and dismay she said she would be unable to help me and that my brother was otherwise occupied. No explanation, no apology. There would be no help, no ride, no support from my mother or my family. Once again I was on my own. I suppose I shouldn't have been that surprised. Often after offering glimmers of hope or help, my mother had a lengthy history of breaking promises to me over the years. Perhaps I just didn't want to see it or acknowledge that she couldn't be counted on. She was my mother, mothers aren't supposed to do that, they're supposed to care. Of course she cared about me, I was her daughter, right?

Irrespective of the mounting evidence to the contrary, though, a small, stubborn part of me still persisted in believing and hoping over the years, that someday the help and emotional support I needed so much would arrive from this quarter. I needed to believe this to go on. Through many incidents over the years, I came to learn to sublimate my suffering for the most part and try not to impose or rely on anyone but myself for anything. So often I was made to feel like I was simply an inconvenience, then as well as now.

So now, here I was once again being an inconvenience and once again I had that feeling of profound aloneness. But this time I really needed help. What do I do ?

Of course I was disheartened, because I really psyched myself to do it TODAY!!!! I sadly called the clinic and told them of my plight. They responded by offering me something unbelievable! They said that they wanted me to be successful in my efforts, and if I could get there in a taxi, they would pay for it! I called the cab company and got there on time. To further support my cause, the taxi driver (of all people), stayed and waited for me, drove me back home and escorted me safely to my front door! She even called to see how I was doing. Such generosity from strangers touched me deeply.

I don't remember the next few days very well, but I believe I kept busy by painting the house, because it was beautiful when I came out of my stupor.

LOOKING PAST THE SMOKE SCREEN

The challenges of being a successful non-smoker were just beginning. As the days wore on, I started to go through all sorts of manifestations, physical, emotional and otherwise. The most profound change was my raging anger...at my mother! All those years of putting a lid on my feelings started to "bubble-up" big time. When she would take me out for drinks, which incidentally, was not helpful at this sensitive time, I found myself unable to contain myself. I let her have it. It was like the cork was popped and every negative bottled up feeling that I managed to contain for years came pouring out. I was shocked at what came out of me...so was she. Up until this point I always tried to keep it light around her for fear of retribution. But now it didn't matter. I couldn't contain it. She'd have to take it.

After a while, I refused to go with her for drinks. Drinking was the main thing I learned I could not do if I was to be a successful non-smoker. She called me boring and a party pooper. So what! At least I was a *non-smoking*, boring, party pooper.

In addition to the anger, came the rise of other emotions with which I had little experience; sadness, fear, shame, confusion and despair. I found my responses to external stimuli to be exaggerated and at times inappropriate but I couldn't help it. Just like a child, I was learning what emotions really felt like. Sometimes it was hard to pinpoint just what it was that I was feeling. One thing was sure, I felt embarrassed to be 31 years old and going through this emotional "kindergarten" of sorts. Many times I wanted to turn back. Many times I wanted to quit. Many times I wanted to hide. But I kept on going. Then my body started to rebel on me. All the toxins from years of poisoning myself started to come out. Many days I felt bad, my skin broke out, my mind was reeling with things I didn't want to think about or remember. It seemed like everything was on overload. I was overwhelmed but all I could do was let it run its course.

I prayed a lot and read uplifting books through this hard time. I meditated and found I needed to cry...a lot. I wrote affirmations until my hand was numb. I'd listen to my positive affirmation audiotapes at night. I often looked at my Wish Board, but now I found that I didn't pray for money anymore. Now, I just wanted to get through the next minute. I just wanted to feel better.

I'd scrape through the day and I'd soothe myself in a warm tub at night. I did this for months. Then one day it didn't hurt quite so much.

I actually tried quitting 13 times before I was ultimately successful. Physician's Clinic was number 12. The tragic and untimely death of my cousin, seeing her in the coffin, proved to be number 13. Seeing the finality of a life did it...for good!

Accidentally, I discovered that my increasing sobriety had become a natural by-product of quitting the smoking habit. I knew I wasn't as fun as I used to be. I was learning how to take responsibility for my life and I was learning how to protect myself from temptation and the bad influences that surrounded me, threatening to pull me back at this tender time. It was shocking for me to realize that among those bad influences was my own mother encouraging me to party with her.

I now understood that I had to keep her at arms' length if I wanted to really be a successful non-smoker and begin to heal my body and spirit. For all her nagging about me quitting over the years, she's the one that made it the most difficult for me to succeed. Her own desire for emotional escape overshadowed her desire for me to be successful. I now had to begin to face the truth that she was not good for me. This experience helped me to realize she did not have my best interests at heart. I had to protect myself...from her!

Avoiding alcohol was tough at first because it was good for so many things, socializing, celebrating, and forgetting. But I found that when I put down the cigarettes, I started to become less interested in drowning my feelings.

Occasionally though, through times of extreme stress or fear I'd sometimes temporarily fall back on my old habits, until I'd regain my sanity. Those times became fewer and fewer as the years went on.

THE WAR OF THE WORLDS

As I had been diligently adopting and implementing healthier behaviors and working with positive concepts about myself, I had to allow for the major changes that were now happening in my life and I just had to go with the flow. At times there seemed to be nothing concrete that I could hang onto as everything seemed to be in a state of flux. The painful world I knew well all my life was changing and I didn't know what to expect from the future. I was scared to go into the unknown. To comfort and reassure myself that this was a normal if not frightening part of the process, I read Ponder's book *The Dynamic Laws of Healing* until the pages fell apart. And though I could read about it, and try to intellectually comprehend it, I was not prepared for what she refers to as "chemicalization." Basically it is when long standing negative thoughts and feelings that have been buried, clash with the new positive input. For me, it was extremely emotionally and physically draining and uncomfortable. In a way it felt like spiritual surgery. Toxic, emotional poison from decades of bad thinking was being released and eliminated from each and every cell in my body. It was frightening and I thought I was having a nervous breakdown. I couldn't function very well and I needed to sleep a lot to escape the pain of it. When I was awake, I seemed to have no control over my emotional nature and I became a confused, crying mess. It was impossible to work and I spoke to no one for at least a two weeks. Who could I share this with that would understand and not try to snap me out of it? If it had not been for Ponder's explanation of it, I probably would've stopped this cleansing and healing process altogether for fear I was losing my mind. But I did not stop it. I did not deaden it with pills or alcohol or psychiatric counseling. I just trusted and allowed it to run its course just as if I had the worst case of the flu I'd ever had. I tried to make myself as comfortable as I could, reminding myself that this too would pass. As bad thoughts and memories flooded my mind, feelings I had long forgotten about my childhood and my parents' divorce came vividly into my consciousness. I had to just let those nightmares flareup, burn, then fizzle, until the wound was cleaned out. I prayed a lot during this time.

Somewhere I read, "Teacher, how long must I remain in the dark?" "Until you can see in the dark." was the reply. I thought of that question and answer a lot during my ordeal. The dark night of my soul seemed pitch black with no apparent way out. I felt totally and utterly lost and alone. I just had to keep on going blindly until I found myself on the other side of it. No one could make their way through that blackness for me. That journey was mine alone to take. It is the journey where I had to face my deepest fears, a journey where I had to face myself.

Eventually the chaotic, fearful feelings subsided and slowly but surely I started to feel somewhat in control once again. After such a purging, things would, at first, feel a little shaky, like whatever changes I went through hadn't "gelled" yet. And, like Scrooge after being visited by the three ghosts, I felt surprised to have made it through alive and intact. After one "chemicalization" it literally felt as though a huge thorn that I had learned to live with was removed, and the resulting void felt extremely foreign. Like I was in someone else's body.

Letting "chemicalization" run its course in my life has always proven to be the right and courageous thing to do. Despite the discomfort, I'll never regret giving myself permission for taking the time to go through it, so that I could begin rebuilding my better life on a more solid foundation. In the end, I found that I was being liberated from long-standing emotional traumas of the past. Yes, this process was painful and frightening, but it proved to very necessary and beneficial.

Inevitably, happier circumstances, new people, or prosperous opportunities would always come effortlessly into my life as a direct result of these cleansing experiences. Because I had done the work to make room for them I could better recognize and appreciate these good things when they appeared.

PART 3: LIMBO

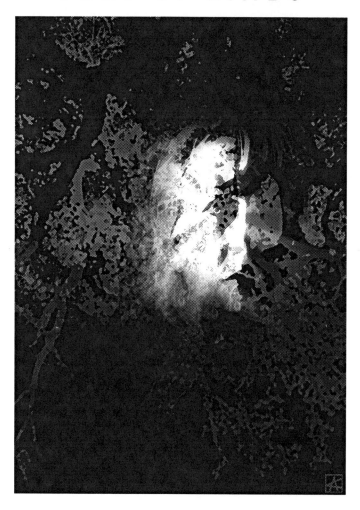

Chapter 5

A wise man builds his house upon a rock – Matt. 7:24

FINALLY ON MY OWN

One day something unbelievable happened. My mother announced she would be moving to a small, rural town many hundreds of miles away. Moving was something she said she would never do. But now, she was finally leaving the big city she hated so much and thus starting the process to let me go. I was at last being given the freedom to individuate from her at 33 years old. This is something I had been struggling, fighting, pleading for since I had turned eighteen! But part of me truly expected and was resigned to the fact that we'd be joined at the hip for life.

Even though I had wanted it, I never really expected to ever get freedom from my mother. On one hand this was the opportunity for the liberation I had been praying for, but it was also extremely frightening because I had lived in this prison of emotional servitude my whole life. I didn't know any other way to live. I felt absolutely alone and clueless as to where to begin or how to proceed without her as a constant focus in my life. In addition, I had to come to grips with the reality that I would never have a healthy mother-daughter relationship with her. Our opportunity had come and gone and now it was over.

My life was now to have a completely new focus. Me. I was finally free to begin the long and difficult journey to rebuild my life as one of health and wholeness. I could begin what I now believe was my own "reparenting" process because literally that's what I had to do. Relearn absolutely everything from the ground up. Emotionally, I was a child, with the inability to cope with life and all its demands and challenges. I had to grow up all over again and get myself the skills necessary to live, not just exist.

LONELINESS & BEING ALONE

In my early years I would rather have had my worst enemy around me than be alone. I couldn't bear the feeling of being with myself…this stranger with a lot of bad thoughts. When I'd suffer a breakup of a relationship the physical manifestations were so profound I could barely function: Depression, inability to keep food down, weakness in the knees. I'd literally waste away just as I had when I received my 21st birthday letter from my dad. When my mother left town and let me go, it was a very big breakup and my collapse was total.

All my life, she had been holding on to me so emotionally tightly that I didn't know how to function without her. Through some weird twist we had become as empathetically entwined as Siamese Twins connected at the soul. Now I was being untwisted. I don't actually remember getting out of bed for most of two weeks although I know I had to have done so. I didn't know or care how I would live, let alone make it to the next day. But the next day did come. And God had given me a small open window…

The night my mother left, I set my alarm for 2 a.m. so I could be there to see her and my brothers off. I felt it was my duty to do so, despite my negative feelings towards her at this point. I mustered as much polite courtesy as I could and made sandwiches for their trip. When I arrived, her house was dark. They had not yet awakened, so I decided to wait and not disturb them. It was cold and I waited for quite some time. I figured this would be the last time I might see them for a long time and I should be as congenial as possible considering the situation. When the lights came on, I went to the door to offer help with loading the vehicle and offer the sandwiches. It turned out to be a very unpleasant scene. I was accused of "lurking in the dark" and I was extremely sorry that I showed up at all. But it turned out that I was there for a reason. Just not the reason I thought.

Everything had been loaded up, but one of her cats simply refused to get in the truck. To avoid capture, she jumped into my car. I was amazed at her behavior because it had been my experience that cats really didn't like riding in cars. And, while I loved animals, I did not want a pet at this time in my life. I did not want the responsibility. I couldn't take care of myself let alone another living thing. But she refused to budge and I had no choice but to take her home. I now had a companion whether I liked it or not.

As much as I wanted freedom from my mother, the departure of my family now also left me with profound feelings of abandonment. In addition, it also had been quite a shock for me to go from the excitement of being on the radio and doing TV commercials to the screaming silence that was now my experience. I was despondent that all the "good times" in my life had now come to an abrupt end, just like that old song *Is That All There Is?* My life had become so terribly isolated. I didn't know where I was or what was in store for me.

This small kitty Tupper, it turns out, gave me a reason to get out of bed in the mornings. We ate together, and at night, she would sleep on the small of my back. She comforted me, and brought simple joy into my life. She's the only one I ever knew who unconditionally loved me and stayed with me through all my tears and pain. She kept me company while I learned how to be alone, be with myself and eventually grow to actually enjoy my own company. She taught me how to be an excellent caretaker of something that counted on me and eventually that care-taking experience was transferred onto myself.

Together, over the years, we learned to trust and love one another. Other relationships would come and go but Tupper, as it turned out, would become my faithful companion for the next seventeen years of my life. Her devotion will always be a cherished part of me.

SOMEONE TO TALK TO

I couldn't handle the challenges I would have to face all alone. I had to find someone who would be neutral and truthful with me, and who wouldn't hold my past against me as I progressed. I just needed someone safe to talk to for once in my life. My search led me to a spiritual counselor named Twilah.

Twilah's home was a peaceful sanctuary. Contented cats and dogs roamed freely on the pristine carpet that was kept that way because absolutely no shoes were allowed. An enormous metaphysical library lined one whole wall of the living room. The plants and fountains lent an air of tranquility and quiet joy to the surroundings. I liked Twilah and immediately felt comfortable in her sanctuary. I was led to a lavender-colored room with a small massage-type table in the center. There were beautiful paintings on the wall and crystals and geodes displayed on the countertops. The smell of incense lingered in the air. I felt I could relax here, something I couldn't say about any other place on earth at that time. I'd be instructed to lie down and she'd place one hand on my solar plexus as she'd encourage me to speak and we'd begin the work of the moment.

Mostly I didn't speak, mostly I cried. I usually was in a lot of pain and felt a great deal of fear by the time I would get to see Twilah. She offered me a safe place to vent and cry and question. She would kindly but firmly offer direction or suggestions that I could choose to adopt or not. She would patiently work with me to get through the momentary crisis and help me discharge the emotional negativity that had a stranglehold on my life with her skills as a healer, remaining impartial and healthily detached while doing so. She never sugar-coated anything for me. If there were harsh realities to deal with, she always spoke plainly and helped me to face the truths that I didn't really want to face. Twilah was the first person I ever really trusted and I took what she said to heart. If there were adjustments to be made with my thinking and behavior, I acknowledged them and did my best to work to correct the problems. I did this diligently, because I did not like the pain and I would do anything to be rid of it. The bottom line was that I always felt better after a session with her.

Although I did not have a lot of money, I managed to scrape together enough to see her regularly at least twice a month, sometimes more as needed. I'd rather do without something myself than be without Twilah when I needed her.

I looked up to her; she had a calm wisdom about her. She possessed a quiet strength that I had never experienced with anybody before. I liked it and felt that I was with someone who I could actually learn from. As I look back, I believe I subconsciously adopted her as a surrogate mother, as I desperately needed some positive role-modeling in that area.

Twilah became an important part of my life and performed the wedding ceremony for my second marriage. She was also there to counsel me at its demise five years later. I appreciated her help and influence. I came to rely on her quite heavily. I really had no one else.

We did have our disagreements though. There was a period of time when I could not see her on a weekday as I had gotten a job that allowed no flexibility with time whatsoever. But I still needed to see her, and asked her for a Saturday as an alternative to my regular time. She refused, saying it was not one of her working weekends. I guess after so many years of seeing her, I felt like she owed me a bit of leeway. There was never any leeway and that's just the way it was. In retrospect, I think rightfully so. She saw so many people and dealt with so much negativity all week, I'm sure she needed a break from it all. But I mistakenly began to take our relationship personally after so many years, I felt she was my family and felt I deserved special dispensation. I did not, and I learned to live with that and allow her time off, learning to deal with things myself in the interim.

Tithing was a way I could show my appreciation and support for the kind of special help I received from Twilah. With her assistance, I began to grow out of my poverty consciousness as well as other false beliefs and methods of behavior. As my life started to improve, I began to modestly prosper and I enjoyed sharing my good fortune with her as someone who had helped me so much. Twilah never asked for it and I viewed it as a small means to help keep someone with her spiritual gifts elevated and uplifted from the drudgery of monetary concerns.

For 15 years Twilah helped me slog through a tremendous amount of serious emotional work. In the safety of her presence and knowledge, she helped me to look at, process and release the mountains of negativity that I had to deal with. There was so much of it and I could not have done it alone.

I owe her an enormous debt of gratitude and she, in large part, is responsible for directing me to where I am today.

RELEARNING THE BASICS

I discovered that there were certain simple, basic things that were good for me to do on a daily basis whether I felt like it or not. They were:

• Eating – This was difficult for me as I found it hard to keep things down when I was emotionally upset and that was a lot of the time. I had to learn to eat what ever good and nutritious food I could afford, to keep up my strength, mental stability and emotional equilibrium. When I didn't, I noticed that my thinking became negative and fearful.

• Moderate exercise – Many times I did not feel I could get out of bed, but I could manage a walk or some yoga exercises. This would also help my mental outlook as well as benefit me physically.

• Releasing Meditation – At the end of the day, I would release the day completely, and imagine myself being washed clean and then recharged. This gave me a sense of hope. I would forgive myself and all who hurt me. My favorite saying became..."We start again." After all my mistakes, I must've said that phrase a thousand times.

• Praying and Connecting Spiritually – This encompassed simply asking for what I needed at the moment, also included writing affirmations, listening to positive tapes, focusing on positive images, reading positive and helpful books—anything that could aid me in eliminating and changing the fearful and negative thinking I had been programmed with. These things were especially useful at times of emotional upheaval and through times of the physical pain of detoxing and breaking free from my addictions.

These simple building blocks were to become the foundation on which everything else was built. It took awhile for them to be integrated seamlessly into my life. But after a while, they became the healthy habits that I could always count on no matter how rough things got.

As I became adept at these ways of living, things of course improved. When my circumstances changed for the better I could then add fun, entertaining and beneficial methods to my "coping toolkit." I made a promise to myself that every time things got rough rather than abusing myself, I'd do something kind and healthy for myself instead. It really didn't matter what it was as long as it did not involve hurting myself or anyone else. Once I changed that one simple thing, I could weather anything, no matter how bad, successfully.

When unexpected or frightening things happened I could now do many things in addition to the basics. If something fearful came up, I'd call a trusted friend. Unexpected work problem, I'd treat myself to a candlelit bubble bath. Relationship problems, see a movie or go to the bookstore. Mother calls, go to the driving range and hit some golf balls—real hard. Simple things really, but they would get me though positively.

Chapter 6

Lead me in your truth and teach me – Psalms 25:5

HANDLING DISAPPOINTMENT

*I*f I had carried my disappointments with me I would have been be so crushed by them I couldn't have functioned. I wanted my daddy's love and approval...I didn't get that. I wanted my mama's love and kindness...I didn't get that. I wanted a loving family...I most certainly didn't get that.

At first when I'd experience a disappointment, I would argue, blame, justify, or beg the person to see it my way. I'd try to turn them around to my point of view. When I didn't get the love or understanding I wanted from the sources I felt it should come from, I punished myself mercilessly and was hopelessly enmeshed in resentment and bitterness. Quite simply, handling things these ways never worked. It took time to learn that people are who they are. Just because they happened to be my mother and father didn't necessarily mean they automatically had the capacity to give me the love I needed. As every kid does, I had an idea in my mind of a perfect family...a mom and dad that were loving, patient and supportive. I wanted that more than anything. I waited and waited for that to come true; I wanted them to really see me. I was sure they could love me if they saw the real me...but they never did, and they never would. There was that moment when I had to realize it would never come to pass and I had to let go of that dream forever. That was a bitter pill, but the truth, as they say will set you free.

What I was left with was exactly where I was. I had to start from that very place. OK, so the "parent hand" I got dealt was down right destructive. OK, so from now on, what I chose to do with my life was up to me and me alone. If I failed it would because of my lack of effort. If I succeeded it would be because of my hard work and perseverance. There would be no one else to blame from that moment on. The responsibility of my life was completely on me. Everything I did, everything I ate, every meditation, every workout, every job, every relationship, every attitude was my choice. I would now be the creator of my life experience and now that the responsibility was on me, I had to take care...of me.

The first thing I had to learn was how to turn disappointments around. If, for instance, a person hurt me or let me down in some way, rather than coaxing them to be different, I'd instead focus on my own life and start fixing whatever needed fixing right there. This was new for me. Prior to this, I would either get too upset to function or get caught up in the other person's drama. Focusing on living my life allowed me the perspective to be functional even if someone else had hurt me, it also did not allow them to take their pain out on me. I noticed that eventually, whatever the other person was going through got sorted out within themselves and I was no worse for wear over it. I guess I was learning not to take things so personally.

During one relationship, I had so many disappointments that I accomplished many things personally. I signed up with a support group to help myself get over my debilitating fear of public speaking and began compiling material to begin writing this book. Every time I got the urge to want to change someone else, I trained myself to look at what in my own life needed tending.

LOSING "FRIENDS" AND GAINING ALLIES

For a person who used to feel connected by sharing and hearing about all the bad things that happened to my friends during the day, refraining from this mode of friendship proved challenging for me. Negative talk was better then no contact at all, I figured. But as I started growing in my new understanding, I began to realize how detrimental this truly was. Many times after a negative mutual "dump session" with someone, I'd feel worse than I did before the call. So when I decided to zip it up about the bad stuff that I was going through and wasn't as open to others' negativity as I had been, something odd began to happen. The "friends" that I thought were so beneficial to me started to fade from my life. I didn't understand it at first, and I felt bitter about the abandonment, after all, didn't I have enough of that already? But the truth was that without the "misery loves company" scenario in play, I just wasn't as much fun to talk to as I was before. And with what I had going on taking up the majority of my time and energy, I actually had very few positive things to say to anybody. Of course, with my change in behavior I became unappealing, and soon people stopped calling. I had to let them go and let them just naturally fade from my life. The consolation was that as they left, it inevitably made way for new more positive people to show up in my life. People who could help me and people whom I could help.

LEARNING DISCIPLINE

Disengaging from the noise and excitement of the world was difficult for me. I didn't want to miss anything. With so much distraction, so much entertainment available I could fill the emptiness with something at all times if I wanted to. But the real work didn't come from the outside. It came from deliberately disengaging and quieting myself down.

At first it took deliberate effort to tear myself away from distraction. I found a soothing meditation tape and every night I would listen, calm myself down, release the day, pray, recharge and in the stillness I would ask questions that I needed answering. Inevitably the answers would come. After a while I came to enjoy these "time-outs." I found them rejuvenating and a source of strength for life's challenges. When I became accustomed to the feeling of connection when I was in meditation mode, I realized that I could go "there" anytime I wanted, even amongst a crowd.

This feeling of connection to the Universe is unquestionably the one thing that has sustained me through all of my challenges. It is a feeling of sublime joy and peacefulness. It is my North Star in a world of chaos and confusion. It has never let me down. It's God to me.

DEVELOPING MY INTUITION

When I was 19, I was so completely without of a sense of direction that one day I pulled to the side of the road and sobbed. I simply didn't know what I was supposed to do or where I was supposed to go. I found it amazing that other people seemed to know this instinctively. They seemed so busy and purposeful. No one seemed to give it a second thought or had a doubt about it. But how did others know? Who taught them?

All I knew is that whatever the capacity was within a person that points the way in life...I DID NOT HAVE IT! I assumed that maybe I simply was born without it. To survive up until now, I had to be the malleable sycophant who had been told what to think, what opinions to have, what feelings to feel. I had no idea what was expected of me outside of this. I felt like a cripple, so I faked it the best I could. I lived this way for quite a while and got into quite a bit of trouble. Without direction, I was at the whim of stronger wills around me. I was vulnerable and open to harm. I needed a compass but hadn't the slightest clue as how to get one or where I would find such a thing.

As I progressed to clean things up and my addictions started to lose their stranglehold on my life, a remarkable thing started to happen. I began to get clear and concise feelings about my life's direction and the next steps to take. Sometimes it was small, simple things. Do things that need doing. Repair something that needs repairing, make things orderly, beautify the living area. This was a real breakthrough for me, as I never had any leadings or intuition at all about anything or anyone before this, or if I did I buried it long ago.

Then it started to get interesting. If, for instance, I needed work, I would meditate about it and let it go. I would be directed to go somewhere, talk to a particular person only to find out that their brothers' wife was looking for a person with my particular skill. This started to happen more and more. It served not only to enrich me financially, but offered me protection as well. One evening, there was a particularly bad windstorm. At about 2 a.m., I was awakened out of a sound sleep and had the overwhelming urge to move my car up the driveway about ten feet, which I did. The next morning I found the large acacia tree in front, which had been there for nearly 75 years, had completely toppled. Had my car remained where it was, it would've most certainly been crushed.

As I trusted this power more and more, it grew more and more. I trusted it for everything large and small, from a parking space in a crowded mall, to finding the right accountant to help me with my finances. At this point, there is not one decision I make without consulting and heeding my intuitive leads. Period. Now, if I do not get a lead I do nothing and wait until I do. It is the compass out of the wilderness; it is the light at the end of the tunnel.

PART 4: PENITENCE

Chapter 7

The still small voice within – 1 Kings 19:12

SEEING THE GOOD IN MYSELF

At one point if someone offered me money to look in the mirror and say "I love you" to myself, there was no way I could have done it. I would've given the money back to them because it would've been a lie.

I really didn't like myself very much. Hate actually isn't too strong a word for what I felt. I figured if I wasn't lovable enough for my parents, I wasn't lovable enough for myself. If something went wrong, regardless of what it was, I would blame myself. If I made a mistake, I was extremely hard on myself for days. I was impatient and self deprecating. I didn't take very good care of my needs or myself. I couldn't buy anything for myself, feeling it was a waste of money. I never liked to have my picture taken. I always saw, focused on, and noticed only my imperfections. I couldn't accept compliments, even if they were genuine. In fact, I didn't feel worthy to receive anything at all.

Turning around this kind of deep self-hatred didn't happen over night. Little-by-little, step-by-step, I had to learn to know, love and accept myself a little more everyday. Instead of being impatient and angry at my missteps and mistakes, I started to adopt a more loving, gentle and tolerant feeling towards myself, like that towards an innocent, small child who was just learning to walk. In fact, I was learning how to be my own best friend, my own parent at this time. If I fell back, I was much more forgiving and encouraging to start again, fresh. I toned down the endless negativity and self criticism and started to praise, appreciate and applaud every little success I made, even if it was something as small as choosing not to reach for that cigarette I wanted so much or even cooking a small meal to nourish my body. At whatever level of my understanding, I just tried to do my best everyday.

Sometimes my best was just getting out of bed. I praised myself for that too.

As I started to notice and appreciate the good and beneficial things I was trying to do, I began to respect myself for every small positive effort I made, a little more everyday. As I praised and encouraged the baby steps I was making, I became stronger. I was finding that I was beginning to work with every facet of myself as a team—the physical, mental, emotional and spiritual—in harmony for the good of the whole organism. Self-hatred and self-doubt began to melt away making way to joy, understanding and appreciation. After much honest effort, it was not hard to say I LOVE YOU to myself and mean it, because I knew I earned it.

COMPARING MYSELF TO OTHERS

With all I had to relearn, adopt, integrate, understand and process, comparing myself to others became one of the most dangerous things I could do to myself. At high school reunions, it was difficult to see classmates' successes, marriages, families and achievements and come home to my own life of challenge and struggle. I couldn't really explain, "Well, you see, for the past ten, fifteen, twenty years, I've been searching, to the exclusion of almost everything else, for myself and a reason to be alive." It wasn't appropriate, and nobody cared anyway.

Generally, it seemed that if you weren't a movie star, rock star, sports celebrity, mogul or wealthy entrepreneur, you were a nobody and didn't deserve attention. If you didn't drive a fancy car or have a big bottom line, you didn't register on the radar screen.

I found TV news magazines, highlighting everybody's big deals, multi-million dollar contracts and super careers particularly stressful and demoralizing. I would have to remind myself, "This is not a contest, this is not a race. This is my life. The only one I have to please is myself. Did I do the best I could today?" If the answer was "yes," I have to be content with that and make it do, even if it looked like I was coming in dead last. If the answer was "no," I try again the next day. If I failed again I would start again, the next day…again and again. It didn't matter to me how many times I failed, tomorrow, I would start again, with a clean slate, a little wiser from what I learned by my previous failures. "We Start Again" became my favorite phrase. I used it a lot. It kept me sane. I learned quickly not to compare myself to anybody. Period.

WHAT TO GIVE

Giving was never really hard for me. When I was little, I gave a classmate part of my Halloween costume so she wouldn't feel left out for not having one. It wasn't really mine to give. My mother was none too pleased and rightfully so. I might have been punished, I don't remember. But I felt compassion for the classmate and was compelled to do something about it.

I was always aware of other people's unhappiness. Everybody just seemed to be so unhappy. My parents were preoccupied with their misery and most adults I came in contact with seemed to enjoy arguing, complaining and gossiping more than anything else. As a small child, I'd dance and sing to my pets, make up rhymes and paint and play with colors. I felt a certain joy just for being alive. I don't know why I felt it was my duty to cheer things up if I could, but I wanted to show people that life could be festive. That's before I got poisoned myself and began to shut down.

Shutting me down was simple enough. If I was singing, Grandma would say, "Stop that meowing." If I had energy to burn and wanted to dance, Dad would say, "Stop that jiggling." or "Can't you find something else to do?" if I wanted to paint quietly in my room. Every single thing I wanted to do, I had to stop doing to make those around me happy. But by eliminating my "annoying" natural passions, I was being eliminated too. Because this meowing, jiggling, colorful, musical person was who I was!

There were exceptions. My grandfather, for one, liked when I danced around the house and referred to me as his "little ballerina." My enthusiastic energy didn't seem to bother him at all. He encouraged me and I basked in his encouragement.

There was another surprising exception to the rule. One of my father's patients was a toy salesman. He came over to visit one day and he brought some of his inflatable monkeys and hula-hoops with him. He was such a happy, joyful and playful individual that I've remembered him all these years after only an hour's visit over 40 years ago! His positive aura was very attractive to me even as a small child and I liked the feeling I got being around that much joy. He seemed to take a genuine interest in making me and my brother laugh. He did not seem to disdain children. I had never experienced anyone like him before and he made a big impact on me. His presence brought cheer into our house and he seemed to genuinely delight in our joy and happiness. Sadly, he had to leave and it was back to the status quo.

Giving was a natural part of my nature. I never felt diminished by it. But in my confusion and because of my own feelings of unworthiness, I was indiscriminate about whom I gave to and what I would give. I tried to accommodate everyone and anyone in need who came into my circle. I just wanted to see some happiness even if I had to create it myself.

Once it came down to a decision to pay my rent or to buy my mother a fox-collared suede coat for Mother's Day. I loved her so much. I wanted to please her and brighten her day. I chose the coat and later scrambled to find money for the rent.

When I did earn some money, I'd buy inappropriately extravagant gifts for whoever was my friend at the time. I didn't need an excuse to give, but Christmas time really proved dangerous for a person like me. I liked giving; it made me happy because it seemed to make others so happy. But at the times I didn't earn a lot, money could be a struggle. Struggle or not I felt it was my duty to make others happy in any way I could. If money was part of that, so be it.

The truth was that I had very little else to give. Underneath it all, I felt I was nothing, so what of value could I possibly possess that was worth anything to anybody else really? Driblets of money here and there were how my mother showed her version of love to me, as did her mother before her. It would've been very easy to become enslaved by this unchallenging, if not sporadic source, for which I could sell chunks of my soul and my freedom, a piece at a time. But of course as a result I would never really know my own worth. Was I worth a nickel an hour or a hundred dollars? I didn't know. As I've grown in my understanding, I now believe money to be the easiest thing to give. It takes no thought or attunement to the person. Time and attention have proven to me to be far more rare and valuable gifts.

There was, however, one person that I never gave to, and that was myself. I denied myself even the basics. I could do without. I wasn't worth it. Others were much more worthy to receive than I was. I was hard-pressed to buy myself anything. A badly needed new pair of shoes... maybe next month. That coat I need to stay warm in the winter...maybe next year, I can get by on what I have. After all, I reasoned, there were others that were much more worthy to receive then I was. If I saw some article that caught my attention, even if I really wanted it, inevitably I'd walk away and put it out of my mind. I could do without.

RECEIVING PRAISE

When someone would tell me "you are beautiful," or "you are intelligent," or "you are talented," it made me very uncomfortable. They obviously didn't know me very well or they wouldn't say such a thing. I'd take it upon myself to "set them straight" with self-deprecating remarks or self-effacing humor. As I look back, I see how mean it was to the "complimentor." I essentially was telling them that their judgment of me was way off. I, in my haste to be "honest" with them was actually being insulting to their intelligence and perceptions. It was rude, not to mention the fact that I blocked any true positivity from coming my way. Learning how to accept and receive anything gracefully was a very big lesson for me.

If someone thought I looked pretty and said so, I'd have to grit my teeth and simply learn to say "thank you," without offering any counter to their remark. This took some time, because it was the direct opposite of what I might have been feeling. I had to learn to shut the hell up, because despite the forceful and persistent nature of my feelings and how convincingly real they felt, I was wrong about myself and life pretty much all of the time. If someone saw fit to give me a gift, I had to train myself to accept it graciously. The universe was utilizing people in my circle as vehicles to get good things to me that it felt I deserved. These were gifts and financial blessings that I had been previously shutting off by refusing to consider myself even worthy to receive. There simply had been no vehicle to get these good things to me. I thought the world was just a mean, punitive and stingy place. In truth, it was my own attitude towards myself that was mean, punitive and stingy. I got what I felt I deserved... either the shaft or nothing at all. Because my heartfelt needs and requests were ignored as a child, I came to believe that people weren't interested in my problems. I didn't want to add to their burdens and I didn't feel I had the right to ask for what I needed.

Opening myself up to ask for and receive help has been the single most difficult lesson I've ever had to learn in my life. One of my best friends once said to me, "You give your friends the gift by asking for their help and allowing them to give to you." When I have felt all was lost, some wonderful, miraculous appropriate help from left field was just waiting in the wings to get to me and always in time if I just opened myself up to the possibility. Perhaps some small gift or kindness I had done for someone previously returned to me when I needed it the most.

LEARNING & KNOWING WHAT TO DO

I'm not a Ph.D. Other than a few months of college, technical computer school and specific courses pertinent to what I do, I have not had a formal education. There have been times in my life where I have felt bad about that. But when it came right down to it, what I needed to know, they don't teach in schools. I have been compensated for that lack in other ways. I have a natural curiosity, persistence and desire. Over the years, I found that if I wanted to know something, I'd either find a book, go directly to the best source I could find, attend a class or seminar, or ask questions to help me find the right avenue for the information I was looking for. I've never been afraid to ask and never been afraid to admit that I didn't know. It has never failed me. I once heard that "When the student is ready the teacher will appear." It has most certainly been true in my case. I've been directed to my "teachers" throughout my life.

I also couldn't discount myself as a good source of information for the practical, everyday answers I needed…if I quieted myself enough to actually listen to the "still small voice within." I found that by keeping my mind clear and emotions calm that I could "find" what I needed to know when I needed to know it. Once I learned how to do this, during my meditation time I'd begin to tune in to and ask for specific directions or answers to a problem in my life. If I followed my intuitive leadings, I was always given the answer. Sometimes the answers were not what I wanted to hear. They might have been regarding a failing relationship or something I had known way down deep inside but was afraid to look at for quite a while. Those insights were always sobering because then it meant that I would have to take action of some sort, sometimes unpleasant or difficult.

In the beginning, I also devised a simple mental tool. I imagined a half circle. The left side was green, the right side, red. Left, green was yes, the right, red was no. I'd imagine a needle in the center where the colors met. I'd simply ask  questions and allow the needle to point the way to my answer. Inevitably it proved to be right on target if I trusted it.

Going by my gut feeling worked as well. If I had a particularly complex dilemma to sort out, inevitably I'd choose the way that gave me a sense of inner peace regardless if the actual doing of it was difficult or not.

Once I made up my mind and knew it was the right thing to do, I was there. At those times when I was overwhelmed with piles of things, I'd play a simple game called "What is it and where does it go?" This was particularly useful when moving, cleaning out large areas to make them orderly.

FEAR AS A GUIDE

The most surprising source of direction though, was in allowing my fears to guide me. I began to realize that my fears were a compass of sorts. If I heeded the fear it would direct me to where I next needed to focus attention in my life. It would point the way to what I needed to overcome and an inevitable healing in that area. These were the big ones:

I was afraid to use my artistic ability and afraid I was an idiot with computers...

> *I enrolled in computer classes to learn what I needed to know to expand on my natural talent. As a result I have earned a very good living doing what I absolutely love to do while working for myself.*

I was afraid to open myself to love...

> *Once I removed the emotional blocks to me doing so, I finally allowed myself to open up despite the fear. As a result I now know without a doubt that I can love and be loved and I don't need a guarantee that it'll work out.*

I didn't know how to have a healthy relationship...

> *I joined a 12-week relationship group headed by a focused and knowledgeable relationship counselor to explore the dynamics necessary for a successful one. As a result, I'm better equipped to deal with relationship issues and able to recognize potential problems as they come up.*

I didn't know about money or investments...

> *I took classes explaining money management. I consulted an advisor to help me understand investing and an accountant to deal with tax issues. Now I no longer fear handling money or dealing with taxes. I've actually come to enjoy reading about business and economic trends in the newspaper.*

I was absolutely terrified of speaking in public...

I signed up for a group focused on the gentle healing of this debilitating fear in individuals. During the first gut-wrenching session, many unpleasant memories and feelings came to the surface to be re-experienced and healed. It was uncomfortable and embarrassing. Although it didn't happen overnight, I became a member and officer in a local speakers bureau…something I never thought possible in a million years.

In every case, where I thought the fear was too overwhelming to continue or even try, I was proven wrong. My fears actually pointed the way to a happier more fulfilling life than I would ever have had if I chose to hide from them. Having the courage to face and overcome my fears has done nothing but expand my life into a much more satisfying journey. It has opened me up to my potential, and I can hardly wait to see the end result of these efforts with my whole self participating in the process. For the first time I'm excited rather than wary about the possibilities and my future.

I may not have gone to college, but I most certainly have had an education. My real education has been in learning about myself and overcoming misery, in fact, you could say I have a Master's in Overcoming Misery. All I ever wanted was a shot at a successful life… successful in terms of my peace of mind, psychological well-being, the ability to love and be loved, and to create whatever I wanted to create. I believe I am doing this now.

PART 5:
SMOLDERING EMBERS

Chapter 8

And a little child shall lead them – Isaiah 11:16

ADDING INSULT TO INJURY

*A*s a little girl I found that playing the piano brought me a lot of joy. I particularly loved Mozart and Bach and was fearless when it came to playing their compositions, even at recitals. At times I found myself inspired to compose my own music.

When I was eight, I was walking to the local shopping center with my best friend. The neighborhood bully was tailing us and decided it would be fun to throw rocks at us. We decided to take a shortcut and climb down the hill. The bully stood at the top of the hill and proceeded to throw rocks. I climbed back up and told him to stop, that someone might be hurt if he continued. Unfortunately, he did continue, and I was the one that was hurt…in my eye. I rolled down the hill and my friend panicked when she saw the blood in my eye. She escorted me home. I must've looked a fright because when my mother saw me she nearly dropped my little brother and screamed for my father. Dad impatiently entered and asked what the problem was. Then he saw my eye. He asked me to cover the other one and tell him how many fingers he was holding up. I couldn't see anything and I told him so. He snapped, " Don't lie to me." "I'm not lying, Daddy." I responded.

The eye doctor was called in and patches were put on both eyes so as not to put a strain on the good one. I was blind for nearly a month. When the patches were removed, I could see but my pupil would be scarred for life.

During this time I had been preparing for a piano concert. It was the "Moonlight Sonata" by Beethoven. Prior to my accident I had been working very hard to memorize that piece; it was lengthy and complex. Once the patches had come off, I had a very short time to resume pra ctice and get up to speed for the concert. I was scheduled to perform first in the line up.

The day of the concert arrived. All the parents were seated, except for my dad. He stood in the aisle with his arms crossed with that same dour look on his face that he always had. It troubled me more now though and I wished I had not seen him from behind the curtain. I was already nervous and his demeanor just made me more so. The emcee spoke briefly and introduced the first pianist…me. I sat down and began to play, but I couldn't get past the first five measures. I choked. The emcee told me to try again. Again the five measures, then nothing. He asked me to try again. Once again I tried, again the same block. I finally ran off the stage in tears humiliated and embarrassed.

Back stage when the pressure was off I could play the soundless piano and it was all there. My piano teacher was a kind and empathetic person. He knew of my accident and how hard I worked on the piece. At the concert's end he gave every one a gold medal, including me.

When we got home, my dad asked me to come into the den. For a brief moment I thought it was going to be a compassionate father-daughter moment. I really needed that with how awful I was feeling. He sat me on his knee and said to me matter-of-factly, " I pay $40 a month for lessons for you. How do you think you performed today?" I ruefully replied, "Badly, Daddy." Then he asked me, " Who do you think deserves the medal?" I was stunned. I couldn't believe what he was asking me and I softly answered what he expected to hear, "You do, Daddy," as I offered him the medal which he took. I became a sad little girl after that and I lost interest in playing piano for a long time. I even forgot how to read notes. Playing for anyone became a phobia for years as I would only play my own pieces if I was completely alone.

As I look back on this as an adult, I see clearly the trap I was in. I was told never to talk back as displays of anger or being sullen were not tolerated. But if I felt I could've been honest without punishment I would've said, "I DESERVE THE MEDAL. I WORKED HARD FOR IT, AND EVEN THOUGH I DIDN'T PERFORM WELL, IT DOES NOT DIMINISH THE EFFORT I PUT INTO IT. I THINK YOU ARE AN INSUFFERABLE SADIST FOR TORTURING A LITTLE GIRL WHO ALREADY FEELS SO BADLY ABOUT HER PERFORMANCE. GO PICK ON SOMEONE YOUR OWN SIZE."

SHAME ON ME

My father loved "roughing it." He'd dress in army fatigues, get supplies at army surplus stores, and played macho games any chance he'd get. Many summers he would pack us into the back of our four-wheel drive, World War II army ambulance, to take the hot, uncomfortable, arduous, slow and sometimes perilous journey to some God forsaken dust hole in Baja, California. In those days the roads were so bad, with boulders, chuckholes and a "washboard" roughness, that it made a good day's travel sometimes as little as 8 to 12 miles! It could also get to be 130 degrees in some of the desert areas we'd visit.

These trips could always get dicey because of Mom and Dad's volatile temperaments. An argument in those close quarters could really make the conditions seem even worse. My brother and I would just lie in the back, look at each other in knowing silence and invent games to keep ourselves amused and distracted as best as we could.

During one visit we stopped at a small town to go into the Mercado and purchase "fresh" produce for the trip. I say "fresh" facetiously, because nothing on display looked or smelled fresh by any means. But the limes, mangos and papayas seemed safe enough. My father led the way into the Mercado. I followed, and then came my mother and my brother. I was wearing a muumuu that my grandmother made out of a garish pink and orange striped fabric. I was eleven years old, shy, reed thin and shapeless with light blue cat-eye glasses.

Moments after we walked in, all activity came to a standstill. Every Latino male turned and stared our way as we walked in. As a few more excruciating moments passed, I realized something even more horrifying; the focus was not my family...it was on me specifically! I could've died right there and then. I practiced my whole life to be invisible. Why was I getting all this attention all of a sudden? I was nothing to look at after all.

Then it became obvious, it was my long hair, it was the only thing I had going for me. In the summer it would get golden with highlights from the sun. Apparently that was enough to warrant this kind of unwanted attention on a young girl. My dad shuttled me out of the Mercado and once back at the truck began to reprimand me for what he referred to as my "flagrant and provocative" behavior, being dressed like that and all. I didn't know what he was talking about. It was grandma's shapeless muumuu on my shapeless stick-like body. Was he blaming me for the attention given me?

As it turns out he was very angry with me. He pulled a black T-shirt out of his bag and made me put it on over the muumuu. I was left in the hot truck as he went back in to finish shopping with the rest of the family. I felt like an outcast, humiliated and embarrassed about the scene that was created because of me. When they all came back, Dad decided that we needed to find a clothing store to buy me something appropriate to wear for the duration of the trip. He selected a long, pink, pleated skirt. So there I was floating in my dad's black tee shirt and the extra large pink pleated skirt that I had to roll up to fit around my waist. As if this wasn't bad enough, I was also directed to hide behind the army ambulance any time a truckload of Latino men passed by, which was often. Needless to say, it was an excruciating trip. I truly felt that there was something wrong with me. This experience gave me the impression that being a girl was something to be ashamed of; that getting attention was bad. I didn't like having to hide every time someone passed by for fear of embarrassing my family further. Somehow I endured the agony of it all and pretended to go on with life. But the experience did all kinds of bad things to me emotionally.

Years later I asked my best friend how her dad would have handled this situation. She said that he would've quickly extricated her from the market and gently told her that she had done nothing wrong; that these men never saw anything like her beautiful golden hair and just wanted to look at how pretty it was. He would've made sure that she was not placed in that position again and reassured her that it was not her fault.

IN BLACK & WHITE

One day I had to stop by my mother's house to drop something off. I walked in on a viewing of old home movies taken when we were kids. This particular one playing was of us on a beach in Baja. My dad and brother were lighting M-80 firecrackers and tossing them on the sand before they exploded. They were having a delightful time blowing things up. I was in the background running towards them to show my daddy something. Apparently, I had just found an exquisite seashell and wanted to give my special find to him as a gift. As I approached Dad with my outstretched hand, he glanced at my gift and without acknowledging it at all turned away and proceeded with his firecracker games. I was left look-ing bewildered and sad as he walked away. But what I saw as an adult was this little girl still holding up the shell up wondering why her daddy didn't like her gift. Why daddy didn't like her. IT WAS A REVELATION!

As I watched this scenario, I realized that the unloving, indifferent treatment I had been experiencing had not been in my imagination. I had been dismissed and discounted and there it was! This was not a daddy's loving behavior to his little girl. This was mean and cold.

I believe that after this and many incidents like this, I surmised that daddy didn't like me because I was a girl. He had much more in common with my brother. I perhaps thought that if I became more like him then daddy would like me too.

LITTLE GIRL LOST

It was never spoken in so many words, but it was made crystal clear to me that daddy did not like members of the feminine persuasion, at least those of his own household. I was never made to feel like daddy's little girl. So I got around childhood by being a tomboy and playing outside with my brother. We built tree houses and dug mud forts. It was fun and I felt safe doing this. He was my best friend.

I never had a Barbie doll; I never played frilly little girl games. When I was 12, my mother decided it was time to take me to JC Penney to buy my first bra. It was excruciating for me because it would be clear to everybody that I indeed was a girl becoming a woman. I couldn't articulate it then but the incident in the Mercado in Baja still lingered in the back of my mind. My development would mean that I couldn't hide as easily. I was scared. I cried and complained, but she really couldn't understand why I made such a fuss about it. The Mercado incident had become ancient history, swept under the rug and buried. Everyone had moved on, apparently, except an important part of me. I fussed because I knew then that everything would change and I didn't want it to. My brother and I would no longer be allowed to take baths together. I now would have to have my own room. We would now be in different schools. I wanted it back the way it was. It might have looked different from the outside, but I felt I was just a mousy little girl trapped inside this developing woman's body. I was not ready for the type of attention bestowed upon me once I turned 15. Up until that time I was happy to be invisible and small. But my sudden profound physical changes made it impossible to continue in that way, and that made me very unhappy.

I managed to get through junior and high school intact because I was so shy, but after graduation it changed. All of a sudden I was getting blatant and uncomfortable attention and lots of it. It just wasn't the type of attention I really needed, but I didn't know it yet. And, although I was not prepared for this, a part of me appreciated the interest in me because it was more than I had ever gotten my whole life. The lure and closeness of sex seemed to offer the affection I had been starving for. Love really had nothing to do with it.

In the early 70's, there was a casual feel about sexual encounters. Because I really didn't trust anybody and never really shared my true self with anyone, I adopted a cold, clinical attitude towards men. I quickly learned that basically when it came to sex, men seemed to be powerless. I held the cards and I preferred it that way. I could take their physical affection and leave the emotional connection for someone else to deal with. I'd simply have none of that. I fancied myself a happy bachelorette and I had my pick of men, young, old, rich, poor. It didn't matter. I didn't think very much of any of them. I figured them all out and they were fundamentally all the same. Poor schmucks!

But on the inside, I was still the tender, little girl that I'm sure was cringing at every leering advance, every improper liaison. Inside, I was still the child begging for love and affection and warmth. All this time I had been drowning her out with my affected hardness and detachment. Her needs had been thoroughly ignored…again and again, except this time I was the one doing the ignoring. I had been taught well.

Chapter 9

A foolish man builds his house upon the sand – Matt. 7:26

THE APPLE FALLS

My mother did little to alleviate my discomfort and confusion about relationships with men or teach me any differently. She never seemed to be there to protect me from Dad's tirades, but was sure to let me know when she thought he "looked at me funny." Of course she hated my father, but it never occurred to her to discuss their problems directly with him or to get counseling of any kind. Her frustration and anger towards him would always be filtered to me, her trained-to-be-captive audience.

After our divorce from Dad, she encouraged my then-boyfriend to "take care" of me as he helped me move into my first apartment. I was astonished that she would suggest something like this and questioningly looked at her as they both broadly smiled at me. The boyfriend felt this edict gave him authority and license to actually live there and "take care of me" in every way. This was not a good arrangement. I was not prepared for this kind of forced intimacy, but did not have the skills or the guts to kick him out. Plus, when I would protest, or need space, he would say, "I promised your Mother I would take care of you." Of course after a few months, when I did find myself in "trouble" good ol' Mom was there to help fix the problem.

It was natural for men to go ga-ga over mother because of her good looks and sparkling charm. But I can never say that she was ever really nice to them. By her own admission she hated men and thought it was amusing to provoke them and leave them hanging. On more than one occasion I would have to rescue her because her flagrant and tipsy flirting would get her in trouble, sometimes potentially serious. It seems that some men did not like to be trifled with. After her divorce from Dad she did have a couple of boyfriends who referred to her as "duchess" and the like. But it was during her brief second marriage to a nice, younger husband that my trust and perceptions of men were further eroded, when he shockingly made a pass at me after a ride home from a family function.

There was this "game" she liked to play when we were out together, called "That's Your Husband." If a sloppy, homeless, drunken, ill-kempt derelict walked by, she would joyfully label him my "husband." What fun. Sometimes I wondered if she really was kidding. So this had been the extent of my education about men.

By the time mother moved away and finally left me on my own, I was in utter conflict and confusion about what I had been taught, what I needed, what was real and how to go about getting what I needed. I didn't know where to begin. Those worries proved to be trivial and would need to be abruptly shelved with what she next had in store for me. Out-of-the-blue, mother suddenly announced that she had a change of heart and she matter-of-factly explained that she needed cash and had decided to sell the "icebox nestegg" right out from under me. I was expected to be out in 3 days or else her deal would fall through. It was made clear to me that I simply could not let that happen.

TRICKLE DOWN EFFECT

Because I had so little time, I frankly had to rely on a higher power to help me find a place to live that didn't require weeks of qualification checking. Thankfully, one of my clients knew of a room addition built for the ailing aunt of the property owner. There was no kitchen. I would have to wash dishes in the bath tub.

My acceptance as a tenant was predicated on whether my cat could get along with their dog. When I heard this requirement, I simply couldn't contain myself and I broke down in tears. When in the history of the world did these animals ever naturally get along? I was done. What to do now?

In a moment of extraordinary compassion, the landlady, realizing the absurdity of her requirement, said that I could stay if I could just please try to keep the cat away from the dog. Done and done! There were worse things than having the dish soap next to the shampoo. I would simply make it work.

Because I had no extra money and so little time to prepare and get help, I ended up moving very heavy things into a van that I borrowed. The only moving man I could find to help me with the piano on such short notice, wasn't muscular and shouldn't have been labeled a "moving man." When he showed up with a rickety truck and an extremely pregnant wife, it became crystal clear that it would be me and not the pregnant wife on the other end of the piano. Frankly, it took every ounce of strength I had.

This sudden rousting from my home took a devastating toll on me in every way. After my mother had moved away, I had just gotten into the rhythm and acceptance of the "ice box" as my legacy, my one safe place on this earth, and was determined to make it work. To be ejected so quickly and without warning forced me into weeks of recuperation, not only from the overly physical exertion but the mental strain and emotional shock as well.

After everything was finally moved, I sequestered myself away for at least 3 weeks in a black depression trying to recover from the whole experience. Eventually, at a very slow pace, I mustered the will to create a makeshift kitchen with a hot plate and a small refrigerator. Every inch of me hurt and my soul was flattened like a deflated beach ball. I had completely lost faith in people. If my own mother could do this to me I felt that I didn't want to run in this rat race any longer. There was nothing here of interest to me.

My landlady became increasingly alarmed at the extent of my lengthy isolation and took it upon herself to do something about it. It was so sweet of her really. Once again here was a stranger looking out for me.

One day she brought me a news clipping of what she thought might be interesting singles events offered in the area. She wanted to see me get out more, meet people. The reality was that I was walking scar tissue. I didn't want to go out, but I agreed to make her happy and make the attempt.

My very first time out from the isolation booth I met Richard. On the happenstance of proximity, we found ourselves being paired up on the thin path of the hiking trail. Actually, it proved to be a gentle, non-threatening way to meet someone. He seemed nice, soft-spoken and even-tempered. I did my best to appear "normal," sublimating my inner anguish and what was now a nauseating terror of people in general. Luckily I still had my tried-and-true modus operandi of emotional distance and personable agreeability as shields to hide behind. I felt I needed those resources now more than ever.

It proved to be a very pleasant day and it became obvious that Richard liked me. He called the very next day to tell me he would be leaving on an extended vacation but would call me when he returned. It felt good to be spoken to so kindly.

When he did return we went on our first date. I was impressed by Richard's emotional composure and total absence of histrionics. He was stable, predictable. It was a refreshing change from the chaos and inconsistency I was used to. To me, at that point Richard seemed like a life raft in the middle of a shark- infested ocean. And this life raft seemed to really like me.

After a lighthearted second date, the pressure to sleep over started in earnest. Richard, I found, could be very persuasive and persistent when he wanted something this badly. I honestly didn't want sex nor was I ready for that kind of intimacy in any way and I said so. I was still reeling from all I had been through. Yet he persisted.

If I had the perspective I do now, I would've seen this forcible behavior as quite disrespectful and unattractive and would've bid him a strong good night right then and there. But I was so needy and frightened of what life could bring and so desperate to belong and feel someone's warmth, that against my better judgement I acquiesced. I simply could not endure even the thought of yet another abandonment.

Within three months we were living together. Though my life raft had now become the small island of security I had wanted so much as a protection from the outside world, there was nothing about this union that felt comforting to me. I felt frightened at how he chose to lustfully leer at me at the times I needed his tenderness. The even-tempered nature proved in actuality to be an absence of what I'd call enthusiasm, compassion or nurturance. The stable predictability in truth was the ability to emotionally hide through mountains of books and lengthy nature treks or simply not be there when he was desperately needed the most.

There were years-long unforgiveness of past girl friends and utter disdain for any show of affection on Valentine's Day because of some past betrayal which was then to be visited upon me in retribution for the slights given him.

So many times I felt nauseous at what I was feeling and learning, but really it was no different than what I had felt and learned before and had come to expect from my own mother and father. Despite these enormous red warning flags within 5 months we agreed to marry because "we had to." Despite the fact that I miscarried, we proceeded anyway. Ironically, the day we were married was the day I hated Richard the most.

On our wedding day, I found that Richard had arranged a "surprise" for me. Despite knowing about my mother's hurtful behavior towards me, he invited her anyway without telling me! When I arrived promptly to the wedding location, Twilah pulled me aside and quietly said "No, we can't start the ceremony yet, we're waiting for your mother." I replied to her, "No, there's some mistake I already have my surrogate "mother" and "family" here. Twilah repeated. "*Your* mother is the one we're waiting for." I looked at her in astonished disbelief, because SHE knew how horribly painful this would be to me! Then I looked at Richard, who was smiling and laughing with friends, nodding knowingly to me. I almost passed out. My mind began reeling and I felt the bile rise up in my throat. The hurt and betrayal choking my mind with the thought, "Do you mean to tell me that we are waiting for the creature who nearly killed my spirit, who if I just think of her makes me want to vomit, who is driving here begrudgingly on the urging of a virtual stranger, and that I will have bury that anguish, hurt and yes, hatred and pretend to be happy to celebrate what should be my happy day?"

My mother did finally arrive, bedraggled, poorly dressed and put-upon from the drive. I swallowed my revulsion the best that I could and went on with the ceremony in a blind fog. I did my finest award-winning acting that day, being as cordial and polite as I could pretend to be. Regard for the guests and a sense of propriety were the only things holding me together. But when it was over and we got in the car, I, in a very unemotional tone simply said to Richard "I want an annulment." I did not, could not love this man. Somehow we did get past it but it doesn't take a rocket scientist to figure out the trajectory of this travesty-in-the-making.

Chapter 10

No one can serve two masters – Matt. 6:24

A WORK IN PROGRESS

The one area in which I excelled was art. I absolutely loved color. How colors worked together was my passion. In school, it was always my projects that the teacher focused on when showing the class how it was supposed to be done. That focus was embarrassing to me because I thought it would alienate me from the other students. It did, in a way. Occasionally I got called "teacher's pet" and "goody good."

Deep down I appreciated the praise because it meant that there was something I was really good at. In high school, my fellow classmates recognized my talents. I would be commissioned on a regular basis to create custom posters for many of them, sometimes even earning a little money as well.

But when it came time to go out on my own, an artistic avenue was not even considered because of the negative response and downright discouragement about it at home. My father actually told me to find something else to do. It was believed I could never make a living at something so seemingly frivolous. So I left art behind and tried to shoe-horn myself into the world without my natural gifts. As I stated earlier, I tried many things; waitress, secretary, house painter, dock rat, film editor, apartment manager, model, voice-over actor, set decorator. At one point, I even thought about going into the police academy or the air force. I didn't seem to fit anywhere. Something was missing.

Because I loved it so much, I thought maybe I could have art as a hobby on the side. After all, I reasoned, "It's not like I would make a living out of it. I would do other things and just have this as an outlet for my creativity." So I taught myself the basics of graphics and practiced on my unwitting "clients" with projects I'd do for free. I learned each and every facet the hard way. On my first printed project I made a mistake in the border and had to scrape the error off 500 printed pages with an Exacto blade. I learned right then and there whatever is on the master actually comes out on the duplicates! It was a great lesson to get right off the bat.

Then one day I got a paying customer. I had no idea what to charge. I actually was afraid to charge. What if it wasn't good? How could I ask money for it? So I opted to charge very little. If the truth were known, I actually would've been more comfortable if I had to pay him for the privilege of doing the job. I had no idea what I was doing…I read books. I had no idea how to work with printers…I asked questions. I had no idea about the supplies or tools I'd need. I faked it. As long as I didn't have to count on it for making a living, it was all right. But now it was getting serious, it involved money…other people's money. By the time I got everything I needed to do the job, I was way in the red. It took triple the amount of time I thought it would take to actually do the work. It was exhausting and the money was no compensation at all. But in the end the client seemed happy and that's all that mattered to me. I was hard on myself after all of it because I still saw only the flaws.

My many employment endeavors and inevitable disappointments came and went as I proceeded to look for my place in the world. My artwork, only in black and white up until now, on the side, was always remaining the stepchild of my life.

One day, I decided to try my hand at just putting colors on canvas. It didn't have to be good. It didn't have to be anything. I just wanted the color back. It had been nearly 20 years since I had done that!

My hand trembled as I tried mixing a color. All the negative comments from the past now flooding my mind. "Can't you find something else to do?" "You can never make a living at it." Then my own mind started in on me. What color should I mix? What color goes with this one? This is ugly. What made me think I could do this? It doesn't matter anyway. While another part of me screamed "Finish it, whatever it is!"

"It" turned out to be the various shades of turquoise and teals of tropical ocean water around an island. No big deal in terms of artwork. A very big deal to me because it meant I hadn't lost my colors!

MY DREAM JOB

When I was eight years old I fell in love with Charlton Heston in "Ben Hur." I didn't know what it was called then, but I also fell in love with what is referred to in film as Art Direction…the power to transport people to another time and place in all its detail. I wanted to do that. I wanted to be the one to make that happen. After my mother left town and I slowly began recuperating and regaining my balance, I eventually decided it was time to follow through on that dream. I was now 36 years old, and it had to be now or never. I signed up as art director for a student film production to learn the ropes. That was the only way a person like me could break into production design. I signed up for computer drafting classes to learn to draw plans and elevations for sets. I took every class and seminar I could that was pertinent to my new focus. I was determined to make it despite the odds and my late start at it. There was also another need that spurred me into action…a burning need to see my name in the credits. It meant I was somebody and everybody would be able to see that. Everybody, meaning Mom and Dad. I desperately wanted to show them that they were dead wrong about me, that I indeed could amount to something without their help or support.

But the realities of set design, props and art direction, as it turns out, were not at all what I dreamed they would be as a little girl. It was grueling, hard work as a below-the-line peon for megalomaniacal directors with miniscule art budgets with which to make miracles happen. It was an intense roller coaster ride of back-breaking work, insanely long hours, then many months off waiting for the next call, wondering and worrying if there would ever be a next call. I lasted about five years before I started to actually dread getting the call for the next painful assignment. My last job in "the business" was as co-set designer of an awards Show. Then, I thought I finally got my big break on a music video for a big country "star." But after many days of pre-production preparation on my part to rebuild a famous saloon for our production, I was politely given the boot as the "star" wanted to fly in her own people from New York. That was the last straw. A thank-you for all my hard work was all I got from it. I took a long hard look at things and one thing became painfully clear; I had to find where I belonged. Enough was enough.

It was now time to quit playing around with my life. It was obvious that nothing I found to do up until then had ever made me as happy as designing and working with color, no matter what any one said. I decided to take the plunge and invest the time, money and effort necessary into developing my artistic talent. I was finally going to put my full focus and attention on my "stepchild."

Computers were now taking over the graphics industry. Doing things the old "hot-wax, paste-up way" was becoming obsolete. Despite my fear of computers and my possible lack of aptitude with them, I felt it was the way to go. I pulled the plug on all my other activities and decided to give it my all. I told Richard of my decision and I asked for his support. At the time he thought it was a good idea.

I signed up for a 3-month, full time, intensive, computer graphics course at a local technical college. I got a student loan, providing the money for the education as well as paying my bills for the duration. During the day, in school, I soaked up the information like a sponge. At night I'd prepare for the next day's lessons. I did not want to waste one precious moment of computer time while I had it. I wanted to end up with a portfolio that would get me work.

In class I excelled. I discovered I wasn't an idiot on the computer after all. I loved every minute of it! I was extremely fortunate to have a teacher who was a rare combination of encouragement, talent and discipline and I found that I thrived under her tutelage.

After graduation, I didn't even have to look for work. My teacher recommended me to an employer and they called me. Within one week of graduation I had my first job with a starting salary of $16 per hour. When I broke the news to Richard, he was in shock because he was making $17 per hour at the time, and he had just gotten a raise!

I was the first in my class to get a job and the first to own my own computer, which I bought with American Express travelers checks. It was the only source of capital that I had at the time. Every piece of equipment was extremely costly. My first system, which proved to be a dinosaur in six months, cost me a whopping $10,000!

Curiously, about this time, Richard was becoming very angry at my progress. When he saw the kind of work I was capable of doing on the computer, he started to realize that his own position at his printing company might be in jeopardy. With what I knew of the industry, I knew his type of work wouldn't go away. But in his mind, somehow, what I was doing became threatening to him.

One day I came home to discover that Richard had torn down the ceiling of my home office and allowed the debris to deliberately fall on my uncovered computer and keyboard. He knew that I had scraped and borrowed to get this machine and dust and debris were detrimental to the delicate workings of the computer, plus, I expressly asked him to protect it. He promised to be careful. The fact that he didn't said a lot about our relationship and how little respect he had for me and what I was trying to do. When I came home to find this sabotage I called him and simply said, "When you come home and find me gone you will know why." My call scared him and within an hour he was home to discuss the problem.

Richard really seemed to be threatened by the advent of computer technology and felt that it somehow would directly affect his ability to make a living. I understood his dilemma, but it wasn't true. I just could not understand why he was thwarting my ability to make a decent living. My inability to consistently do so had been an issue all through our relationship and now I was doing something about it. My work would've benefitted him too. This incident proved to be the beginning of the end of our already fragile marriage. But I was now on my way to becoming an income-producing woman, doing what I loved to do. It was the single best decision of my life and has sustained me even to this day.

I don't know if my work was actually the last straw with my marriage as there had been other major problems all along. But it certainly helped to contribute to its demise. Perhaps it was because I was changing, taking charge and thinking for myself finally. Richard, for all his complaining, liked me better when I was compliant.

When we separated, though, I now at least had the skills and the potential to earn a living for myself. And little did I know at the time that I would be needing to do just that.

PART 6: PYRE

Chapter 11

The truth shall make you free – John 8:32

CONTEMPLATING THE UNTHINKABLE

When I wasn't ill, the only other legitimate reason to visit my Dad was for a special day like Father's Day or his birthday. It usually ended up with us around his dining room table with a bottle or two of wine and him pumping me for information about my mother and brothers. I knew what he was doing, but I complied because I desperately wanted a sense of closeness with him. It made me feel like he cared about what I had to say and I wanted to please him. But at its core, it was nothing more than an empty exchange of useless information. I'd usually feel bad afterwards. Many times, I should not have been allowed to drive home.

My mother was a different story altogether. When we were little she could be so much fun, she seemed more like a playmate than a mother. When things were going her way, there was no one more agreeable, charming and sweet than she was. Her radiance could light up a room. But any hint of negativity, criticism or a perceived slight could switch off that radiance in a instant and "Mrs. Hyde" would come out. Her inconsistency scared me.

Over the years I had become so adept at reading the warning signs of one of these "episodes," a certain curve of the mouth, a look in her eye or an upraised eyebrow, that I could sometimes forestall the inevitable unpleasant transformation by fawning over her in some way. Sometimes placating her in this way worked, at other times it did not. Caretaking her extensive emotional needs, though, was a full time job, which included but was not limited to; being her psychiatrist, maidservant, gal pal, drinking buddy, whipping boy and handyman. Unlike my father who liked talking about himself, my mother enjoyed going into hourslong detail of how everyone else had done her wrong over the years and I was expected to listen. No matter how I would try to change the subject inevitably it would always end up back there. It was futile and I'd be trapped. Getting married and moving away did little to ameliorate the problem, as it turns out. There were times when the manipulated helplessness was so well acted that I'd drop everything and fly down to her to help her through one of her crises and to help facilitate her "letting off some steam" via drinks or a quickie trip to Vegas. My first husband saw the dilemma right away and decided to defend me by writing a scathingly honest "family update newsletter" encouraging her to buzz off and leave me alone. At that moment he was my hero. He did for me what I couldn't do for myself. Unfortunately, the results didn't last long. After our divorce, when I felt I had no other choice other than to move back home to Mother, our extremely close proximity proved to be so grindingly uncomfortable for me because it was becoming difficult to hide my true feelings. At least when there had been some distance between us, it was easier to pretend that I loved her. The undercurrent of loathing and mistrust, that I could never face or admit to, could be safely hidden and denied away. In person this was harder to do and my unconscious guilt about that kept me hopelessly enmeshed in the emotional web.

For years, this was the scenario with my parents. Of course, I always hoped that things would change. I hoped that my parents would one day come around and become the loving people I wanted them to be. This couldn't be all I'd get after all. Where were the love, the support, and the guidance? When was it going to materialize? When was the selfishness going to end? The painful truth was NEVER!!!!!!!!! This was the parent hand I had been dealt and I had to face that fact. They were toxic to my growth. I found myself giving some serious thought to emotionally divorcing my parents.

THE BEGINNING OF THE END

The untimely and tragic death of my 32-year old cousin proved to instead be the death knell for what was left of my sense of family. My mother called one Sunday morning to tell me the awful news. My cousin had been on Spring Break from medical school and lost control of her skis. She slammed into a tree, lacerated her liver and was dead within hours of her accident. My aunt was on her way to go identify the body of her only daughter. Mother and I cried together over the phone.

Other than my grandparents, who lived a long and full life, I had never experienced a death of a loved one like this. I took for granted that she and I would share our lives and laugh about our whacked out family when we got old. She was the closest thing to a sister that I had…and now she was gone…forever. I felt an arctic loneliness. I felt abandoned. I was the only girl left to deal with these insane people, the only other girl who knew the truth about things…now gone…dead.

I was inconsolable. If there ever was a time I needed my family, THIS WAS IT!!!! I found that I didn't care about any of the weirdness or dysfunction or separation, this was a serious family tragedy. I needed my family. I needed help through this time. I was devastated. I NEEDED MY FAMILY!!!!! ANYBODY, PLEASE!!!! HELP ME!!! Certainly, if there was anything that could pull a family together, this kind of tragedy was it, I thought. Certainly they'd be there.

I was grief-stricken. I needed to call my dad to tell him what had happened. I needed my daddy to help me through my pain. I called him, but to my astonishment, the voice on the other end of the phone line laughed coldly and asked, "So what did she do, kill herself? How'd she do it?", laughing sardonically. My jaw dropped in disbelief at his callous remark. Incredulously, I replied she was killed in a freak skiing accident. He was dispassionate about all of it, and I realized, full on for the first time in my life, with great clarity, just what the hell I was dealing with— a cold, unfeeling, unloving and cruel son-of-a-bitch. I was in shock at his demeanor and my realization. There would be no support from this quarter.

On the other hand, Mother and I talked many times over the next few days, making arrangements to go to the funeral up north. I had no money at the time so she said she would fly me up. I would meet her there; we would stay in a hotel and go to the funeral together. Afterwards I would go to her home for a visit with her and my brothers for a few days. I felt connected with the support I was feeling from her. I needed it badly.

Then things changed. The day before we were to leave, she called to tell me that she would not be attending the funeral. I would have to go alone and represent our side of the family. I pleaded with her, "This is your sister's child. This was your niece. YOU CAN'T NOT GO! You have to be there for your sister, for me. It's not like Grandma, who had a long life and left when it was time. This was a young woman taken in her prime, before her life even started. "It's unthinkable. You must go." She flatly stated that her sister had not formally invited her. I asked her what she meant by that, explaining that one didn't get a formal invitation to a funeral. My aunt had the grisly task of identifying her daughter's body and she had to be beside herself with grief. "What do you expect her to do, give you an engraved invitation? It doesn't work that way. You find out, you get on a plane, you get there, you be there for people, that's it!" She explained that she had only been told to come by my aunt's boyfriend and that wasn't good enough! She said she wasn't going... period. I was reeling! Both parents unavailable! This was a nightmare.

I had to go to my cousin's funeral alone. I truly felt ashamed of both of them. When I arrived in town, I was taken immediately to the church where the services were to be held the following day. It was a magnificent Russian Orthodox Cathedral. As the massive doors swung open, I was struck at the movie set-like production with all the gold, the incense, the icons on every wall...it was overwhelming. I was in awe of the spectacle. There, in the center of this cavernous, gilded edifice was the lonely, bent figure of my aunt, crying her eyes out over the open coffin of her beloved only daughter, my cousin Sasha. She was inconsolable. When she saw me, she fell into my arms and sobbed, "My precious child, I want to go with her. Why didn't God take me instead?" I had no answer. The scene was too much for me. I was overcome with the emotion of it all. I couldn't speak.

Somehow we left and got back to my aunt's home. The first thing she asked me when she composed herself enough to speak was "Where is your mother? I need her. I need her here now! I can't get through this without her." It was my grim task to tell her that none of my family would be attending.

The aftermath of that bombshell was beyond description. My aunt dropped to her knees and sobbed, "I know your mother and I have had our disagreements over the years, but I will take all the blame for all of it on myself, I will grovel before her, I will kiss her feet, but I need my sister now, please get her here. If it's the money I'll pay for a car or a flight, I'll do anything to have her here. Please make it happen and get her here!"

Of course within the next few minutes I was on the phone with my younger brother who lived with mother at the time. I asked him to get her to come to the phone. He did, and I commenced to beg her to come. "Mom, I need to make you understand, you are needed here. Your sister needs you now; she's in very bad shape. You have to get here, by car or plane...the funeral is at 10 tomorrow. Please get here; you don't understand how serious it is." "I wasn't invited," she flatly replied. I stated, "This is not that kind of a thing. You are needed here!" She started to cry, left the phone and handed it back to my brother, who said, "Now look what you've done, you've upset Mother and you've made her cry. Why don't you just leave us alone, you bitch. I'm putting my foot down, we're not going and that's the end of it. Leave it alone." Somehow this tragedy had been twisted to become all about Mother's feelings. Everything else was secondary. How was this even possible? I was in horror.

I had to break the news to my aunt that her sister wasn't coming and that it was because she hadn't been asked properly. It was a hideous task. I didn't know what I could do to help her, as she was so distraught. I assisted her to bed and I could hear her crying all through that long, fitful night. My aunt did try to call my mother repeatedly throughout those long hours but the phone just rang and rang. She refused to pick up and that was that.

My guilt over my family's behavior was immense. When I awoke the next morning, I found my aunt's house empty. In my confused thinking I believed that she and my remaining cousin had purposely left me behind as a fitting punishment for my family's grotesque behavior…and deep down I thought…rightfully so. This is what I had come to expect from my family. But it wasn't that way at all. My cousin was downstairs cleaning the car after he had already taken my aunt to the church to prepare for the funeral. I was so relieved and thankful they had not left me.

The church was filled with hundreds of people who showed up on short notice from near and far, which made my own family's absence even more obvious and abhorrent. I didn't want to believe this nightmare was happening, so every time those great doors opened for latecomers, naturally I had to look to see if it was going to be my family. I prayed it would be my mother. I never prayed about anything so hard in my life. Of course, she never did show and my heart was broken and filled with shame.

Afterwards at the reception many people came up to me to inquire as to the whereabouts of my mother, "Wasn't she the aunt?"

The worst was when the priest came up to me asking me why wasn't she there. I lied and said she was ill. I could've crawled in a hole and died. It was one of the longest days of my life. I truly learned shame that day.

After the services, my aunt and I drank Russian Vodka to drown the pain and cry together at her home. Among the papers on her desk was a dry condolence note from my father. There was no acknowledgement at all from my mother.

During the course of our tearful conversation, my aunt wanted to know how I was doing in general, and after a period of sharing, she then inquired about a rather large piece of property that my grandmother had given to my mother many years back. I recalled the property and explained that Mother had sold it the previous year. My aunt's expression became one of shock as she gasped "What do you mean she sold it?" "Don't you realize that your grandmother put that property in your name too, as a failsafe, so your mother wouldn't sell it so easily when she wanted cash?" My brain was spinning as I tried to wrap my mind around what she was telling me. Then as I composed myself, I began to remember the rather low key request from my mother during the previous year regarding a signature she needed on a particular document...my signature. She told me that if I were to sign it she would have the money she needed and she would generously give me $5000 to tuck away. One caveat was that I was not to tell my husband Richard about it. Although, I was uncomfortable with the secrecy, as always, I did as my mother asked without question. The true nature of the document, or that the property had been meant as my grandmother's legacy for my future, was never explained to me and I didn't know enough to ask about such things. Now, in a blink of a tear-filled eye, I was beginning to understand what it all meant.

When it came time to fly back home, I had to make a decision on whether to proceed to my mother's house for the visit we had discussed. She most certainly would want to hear all about the funeral and the impact her absence had on the proceedings. I could just see her relishing every juicy detail that I would be expected to regurgitate while being offered a few drinks. After a few moments of deliberation, I decided to pass on that little excursion. I found that I did not want to speak about it to her at all. I did not want to drink with her. There was nothing to say. I just wanted to go home. Something apparently had profoundly changed in me that day.

I now could see my parents, who had directed every misstep of my confused excuse of a life with their anger, their punishments and their deceptions, in their full glory. Their ill-informed opinions about me, about others and about the world, their misguided, twisted perceptions about almost everything coming into full and undeniable view.

That day I saw my parents in the glaring, unblinking light of the truth of their actions. I DID NOT LIKE WHAT I SAW. I was in horror at their cruelty, selfishness and callousness. Something else became clear to me…I did not just lose my cousin that day, my whole family died to me as well.. I had just become a deliberate orphan. I may not have known who I was, but I certainly knew who I wasn't. I was not like these people nor would I ever be.

As I drove home from the airport, one phrase kept appearing in huge letters on the blackboard of my mind, YOU ARE FREE. You are free…of their distorted vision of you and of trying to please them. Free…of contorting yourself to fit their mold. Free…of adopting their likes as your own and of hating things and people because they do. You are free…of their fear and of placating them. But most of all, you are free…of their way of thinking. YOU ARE FREE! A part of me was soaring with the possibilities of what that could mean. But then I also had to realize that it would mean that I'd be on my own…completely. That was an extremely frightening scenario to me. It was the greatest unknown.

I argued with myself. After all, wasn't a dysfunctional family better then none?" I had to answer…NO, my mind focusing on my father's cruel laughter and my mother's selfishness. The dreams that I had clung to for so long were quickly dissolving into vapor. Dreams that they might change, that they might come around some day, that we might be a loving family…gone. The true scope of this reality now fully gripping my mind and my heart. It was over. I had no family—I never really did. I came home to my husband a changed woman, a grieving woman. The grief and depression would last a long time and its sublimation would ultimately cost me my marriage.

KICKING THE "MOMMY" HABIT

To put it plainly, my mother had been using me as her emotional repository from early childhood. I really didn't know any other way of behavior with her. But this experience at my cousin's funeral profoundly changed something within me. It had given me the briefest moment of clarity away from her influence. That brief moment was all I needed to change things forever…if I had the guts to seize the opportunity.

Predictably, her call came the day I came home from the funeral. She wanted to know the details of what happened. I found that I was so sickened from everything that I did not wish to speak to her about it and I told her so. She told me to call her back. I found that I did not want to. Prior to this we talked almost every day, sometimes more than once a day. It was my place to listen…for hours, whether I wanted to or not. That, after all, is what I had been born for. The next day, I was surprised to find that the feeling did not leave. I still did not want to talk to her about it. She called again.

This time, she flat out came and asked me why I hadn't shown up to her house after the funeral. I replied, "Because I was so devastated by the whole thing I thought it was inappropriate to have drinks at your house and rehash the experience. It was too painful and I couldn't do it."

Then I came flat out and asked her the question. "Why didn't you show up? After all the calls, and the begging and the pleading. You knew you were desperately needed there, and yet you didn't see fit to come. I needed you, your sister needed you. Why didn't you come?"

Her reply floored me. "Because I hate my sister so much I would've jumped on her back and thrown her into the grave too!" I almost fell off my chair in disbelief!

Oh my God...THIS HATEFUL BITCH WAS MY MOTHER! This is the one who, when she wasn't bemoaning her life, was touting positive thinking and self-help spew. Mother or not, I wanted nothing to do with this person. I hung up on her.

Now the years of her "smotherly love" training were pressing on me. I had never hung up on my mother before. Our fights, no matter whose fault, would always end up with me calling to apologize. That was the formula; She's angry, I apologize; she's upset, I apologize, I get angry, I button it up. I apologize for even thinking it. I was always apologizing. Now once again, it was coming time for me to apologize...or else. I rushed to the phone to dial her number...I paused. Or else what? "Or else she would withdraw her love from me"...I explained to myself. So what if she does? "Well then, I would have no mother." I further explained. What's the difference from what you have right now? "Nothing," I thought matter-of-factly.

My hand was ready to dial the last digit, again I paused, my hand was shaking like an alcoholic in need of a drink. I couldn't push the last number. Something held me back. I put the phone back in the cradle and I let the moment of guilt pass. I got busy working on an intricate model I was building for a school art direction project. I let myself get lost in it, in every detail of it. I wanted time to pass. The phone rang; I did not answer. I simply did not want to talk to her.

So there it was. The truth. The truth was that I no longer cared if

Mother actually did withdraw her love from me, as she had threatened to do all these years. I found that I didn't want it. What she was doing wasn't loving in any way, shape or form. Her capacity for cruelty and selfishness was beyond my imagination and I would lose nothing of value if I just let her go. I could not honor her by allowing this behavior to be okay by me. It was not okay. I had to let her go for my mental and emotional health. Saying it to myself was one thing, actually following through was a different story.

My shaking hand reached for the phone many times for the next couple of weeks, the guilt and childhood training seemingly getting the better of me. But as before, something prevented me from completing the call each time. Every time I put the phone down I became a little stronger, and letting go became a little easier. Then I found that weeks had passed, weeks became months and months became years. There were minor superficial communications between us and one particularly ugly call where I begged her to release my younger brother from his belief that the responsibility for their funeral inattendance was totally on him. I asked her to make it right for her children who had to go on in this life. She, in an harsh and nasty tone, told me that I knew nothing, she was fine now, I was the child and I was told to "have a nice life." But even with that fleeting ugliness, it was nothing like the choking stranglehold that we shared before.

Moments of confusion, guilt and sadness did surface around Mother's Day when everyone celebrated their wonderful mommies with a nauseating whirlwind of hearts, flowers and mushy sentiment. To be respectful I did send cards, but they were carefully screened to avoid misleading or hypocritical verbiage involving the "L" word. The same was true for birthdays. Conversely, I was not comfortable receiving things from her on my birthday and asked her instead to donate the flowers or whatever to her local hospital. Yes, it was unpleasant, but it was the best that I could do, considering.

Despite these awkward moments, I found something amazing happening to me. I did not die without Mother's love and influence. I became stronger. I individuated from my mother. I began developing my own opinions and tastes. I learned to think for myself and started to heal myself emotionally and spiritually. I developed my artistic and freelance skills and began to see what I was really worth. I did not die without her love or her money. I learned to take responsibility for myself and was honest with myself about my needs. I started to live. It was the best thing I ever did for myself. Otherwise, I would have been destined for a life as her lap dog.

What I had really done was the unthinkable...I had emotionally divorced my mother. Another one was to follow as my longstanding mindsets and belief systems were now being challenged and changed.

To complicate matters, I found that Richard did not believe in the mourning process. I was expected to be up and at 'em way too soon after this enormous dose of reality. So I found myself crying during the day, and having to pretend I "was over it" when his car pulled into the driveway at night. But what he didn't realize was that by not allowing me to grieve as I needed to and getting his love and support in that effort, he prolonged the process for both of us. Inevitably the strain of our incompatibility ripped this already fragile gauze to shreds.

In retrospect, I couldn't help but be preoccupied with incomprehensible pain from which there seemed to be no relief. The world I knew had been turned upside down. Richard did not have even the slightest sense of compassion or sensitivity to deal with any of it. I and my family brought so many complications to the marriage, even healthy persons would've struggled. I do not fault Richard; he needed someone much less complicated.

One day, after many gruesome months, I came out of my fog. My grieving was finally over and I woke up to realize that I didn't have a real partner and I never would. He was okay with the better but not worse part of marriage. And I had changed. What I could previously tolerate could be tolerated no more. What never should've started was now finally over.

Chapter 12

Come to me all who are heavy laden – Matt. 11:28

SURVIVAL

With my experiences from the funeral, I now realized that I had no family I could count on; maybe I never did. I would have to go through a divorce from Richard…one of life's most unpleasant and difficult challenges, completely alone. With divorce details, complications and practicalities now consuming my energies, I had to be content being a background graphic arts production person. I knew I could do better than the mundane tasks I was being given to do, but my bosses were flexible and I was just glad to have a job that produced a regular income that I could count on. Plus, it also afforded me valuable, hands-on experience with this new technology that was taking over the industry.

For two and a half years I worked part time at the company, also freelancing and taking on temporary projects on the side. I was paddling as hard as I could just to barely keep afloat, all the while learning and getting good at what I was doing. It seemed that I was riding through the months of divorce issues and all its heartaches and challenges on this little boat of my work.

When the bottom dropped out of the real estate market, so too, did my job, as our primary clientele were big real estate and banking concerns. Recession was in full swing. The only place hiring was a calendar shop. It was the most excruciatingly boring work I had ever done, but it paid the bills. To add insult to injury, the boss was a hotheaded screamer who regularly took out his bad moods on his subordinates. He also did not believe that a woman could really operate a computer. I showed him that he was wrong. But his doubt made my job much more difficult.

One day the printer called and said one of the employees from the night before mixed up the dates on a few of the calendars. They were scheduled to go to press and he asked if I could come over to fix it. Roger, the boss, was nowhere to be found and I was told to keep this dilemma under wraps so as not to upset him.

I went over, fixed the problem and ran right into Roger as he was pulling up in his car. He asked what I was doing there. I brightly responded, "They just had a question about something and I was on my break, so I thought I'd just come over."

He wasn't buying it. He stormed into the print shop and just started yelling at everyone at the top of his lungs. He could really go ballistic. I really felt sorry for the guy who made the error in the first place; he was really going to get it.

Back at the main shop everyone had heard about the blowup, so they were all walking on eggshells so as not to incur Roger's wrath upon themselves. I stayed late doing cleanup on the other erroneous calendars that had to go to press the next day. When Roger came in and saw what I was doing, he started screaming again, but now it was directed specifically at me! I couldn't believe it! I had just bailed him out and was working late to fix someone else's mistake. I did not deserve this.

I stewed over this maltreatment until I felt like I was going to implode. His girlfriend came in and I told her that I thought he had been tremendously unfair to me. She agreed and said I ought to do something about it. I wanted to, but he had left for the day.

As I got in my car getting ready for the long drive home, I realized that I was so upset I couldn't drive, it was like holding onto a hot coal. I spotted a pay phone, got out and made the call to Roger. I told him, "I did not deserve to be yelled at today. I was trying to help the situation. You have to know that if I had made a mistake I most certainly would've fixed it for free and would've taken my lumps too. There was a moment of silence. Then came his deafening blast. "YOU THINK THAT WAS YELLING, YOU HAVEN'T HEARD ANYTHING YET! ALL YOU PEOPLE ARE INEPT AND ARE COSTING ME MONEY! I SHOULD FIRE THE BUNCH OF YOU!"

He was so loud I had to hold the receiver away from my ear. Instead of feeling agitated, though, I became very calm. I hung up on him and proceeded to drive home almost in a trance. Screaming, angry people did that to me. Just that morning I was placed in charge of designing the party invitations and I had brought in the decorations for Roger's Christmas party. Now I was contemplating leaving and never coming back.

All through the night I wrestled with myself on what to do. By morning time I still didn't know. Then I did something that let me know what I needed to do...I simply went back to sleep! I guess I quietly quit that day. Of course it would mean that now, with only four days before Christmas, I would not have a job. But it also meant that I was not going to continue to allow myself to be screamed at or disrespected like that again. I believed that I deserved better.

COPING WITH FAMILY HOLIDAYS

One unanticipated by-product of my decision to quit, was the spectre of yet another lonely Christmas. Not that there hadn't been many before this.

Holidays, in general, while growing up were sheer hell. In fact, I don't remember a single holiday that wasn't fraught with tension and arguments. While other families had traditions that were comforting and joyful, we had door slamming and yelling.

As I mentioned before, the most memorable one for me was the Thanksgiving when Dad announced to everyone at the table that I was a mistake and should've never been born. That goes down as the biggie for me.

But, in general, the forced togetherness of a family who didn't like each other too much was an unendurable torture and, inevitably, something had to blow. Any simple thing could trigger it. One Thanksgiving my grandmother made a remark about the turkey skin, saying it would be the closest thing to a fur coat she would ever get. We kids thought it was funny, but apparently there were sensitivities about this remark and soon it blew up into a full bore, door slamming scream fest. So much for being thankful.

After my parents divorced, our holidays further deteriorated, not that it was a bad thing. On many holidays I found it less stressful just to work and avoid the whole carnival. It was simpler that way. I may have had a sense that there was something missing, but not having anything to compare it to, I just didn't know any better.

Every year about mid-November, though, I'd start to feel a palpable trepidation about the big three: Thanksgiving, Christmas and New Year's Eve. It was like running the gauntlet. A part of me didn't want to participate for fear of the inevitable guilt and potential for turmoil these so-called "festive" occasions could instigate. But once I divorced the family I realized that I would have to be responsible for my own holiday experiences from that point on.

Of course, some holidays were lonelier than others. Circumstances of timing, like leaving Roger's employ, or health issues, created a certain isolation that was challenging, to say the least. It was hard not to feel sorry for myself. I wasn't an ungenerous person. I loved to laugh and make merry just like the next person, but you can't divorce your husband and parents, quit your job, go through all the emotional aftermath and not expect to have a lonely holiday or two. Before that at least I had my illusions. Being alone at these times when other families were gathered together, all cozy and warm, was a bitter pill at times, but my emotional health demanded it and temporary loneliness was the price I was willing to pay. I trained myself to look at it as just another day.

In time, through good friends, I learned what holidays were supposed to be like. I got to experience the real sense of family I had never known. There was laughter, love and warmth. I must say it was a shock for me to see the holidays come and go without a single argument or altercation between family members. People left still liking each other!

Eventually I took a proactive approach to the holidays for myself, making sure I was with friends on these days. Sometimes I would host for people who found themselves alone like me and we'd all get together. Once I let go of expectations of what I thought the perfect holidays should be like, I could actually enjoy them whatever they turned out to be. I realized I could choose how they were going to be, regardless of what was going on around me.

DIVING INTO THE DEEP END

Within two weeks of leaving Roger's employ, I was forced to start my own business. I say "forced" because no one was hiring at that time. The economy was very bad and wasn't going to get better any time soon. It was an especially poor time to find myself with no income and no capital; only bills and a high mortgage payment. It seems the only things I did have going for me was my artistic skills and the absolute necessity to make it happen.

I created a flier of my work and circulated it around to every print and copy shop in the area. Within the first week I had my first client. It was a small logo design job for only $35. I would've liked to have had the check framed but frankly I needed the cash. I knew I had to do better then this and quickly. Mortgage time came around, I didn't have enough money to make it, so I resorted to a cash advance on my credit card to pay the bill. What I really needed was a miracle. By week two I caught a break. A public relations person saw my stuff and he hired me on the spot to do design work for many of his clients. His business kept me alive and I was grateful. Soon others saw my work and I slowly started building a client base of steady customers. Occasionally, I was even making enough to pay the bills.

I was working all the time; nights, weekends and holidays. I took any job that came my way, large or small. Because I knew how frustrating it was to me when people didn't follow through on their promises, I made it a point to deliver when I said I would deliver; keeping my word and doing my best would be my trademarks. Then, two things started to happen. I started getting to be more proficient at what I was doing and through my clients I started to know the feeling of being valued and appreciated. I was finally contributing to the world in a positive way. Not only was I learning how to earn a living, I was learning how to receive honest praise and appreciation for my work too. Actually, I was learning what it felt like to be loved. Yes, it was challenging and difficult at times, but it was a formula that finally made sense to me. I could do this.

Chapter 13

The former things are passed away – 2 Cor. 5:17

ONE LAST STAB WITH DAD

After a four year separation from my dad following my cousin's death, he called one day to get my brother's phone number. All this time I had lived without verbal communication with either parent for most of those four years. I had come to terms with my cousin's death, the absence of my mother in my life, and had my hands full with the divorce from Richard. I was growing up the hard way.

During our conversation, much to my surprise, I found that I didn't care if I had my father's approval or not. When he asked me why I hadn't called him I said that his callous remarks and behavior at Sasha's demise had been unacceptable to me. I went further to tell him that his fear tactics employed upon us as children were not the productive method of discipline he believed it was. It caused a lot of damage that I had been coping with for years. I did not tell him that I had been in "therapy" nearly 15 years to get over his dysfunctional parenting, as he did not believe in God or therapy of any kind. A part of me hoped he would acknowledge what I was telling him and maybe even apologize, but as usual, it fell on deaf ears. I also told him that I had not spoken to my mother in all this time, that I had gotten a certificate in computer graphics and had started my own small business. He seemed very surprised at my accomplishments and his comments sounded like he expected very little from me.

On his first visit with me after our "reunion" call, he candidly admitted that he "had written me off." It made me sad to know that while I was going through loss and grief and emotional struggle by myself, my dad's first inclination was to write me off. Despite its hurtful nature, I let that comment pass, as I was relieved to have at least one parent back in my life. I didn't want to rock the boat.

At first Dad seemed uncharacteristically congenial. I had never seen him like that. He acted more like a love-struck suitor than my father. Somehow I had become interesting to him. He was visibly impressed with my efforts and said he wanted to do something for me. I was stunned because I knew better then to ask him for anything. But he insisted on helping me with a piece of equipment for my business. I appreciated it on many levels. First, the fact that he was helping me at all, after expressly saying he wouldn't; second, because starting a business with little capital during a recession was difficult and scary; and third, because the divorce was taking its toll on every area of my life.

For a time I was happy with our new adult relationship. My improved self-respect and communication skills really seemed to be working for a while when dealing with Dad. Of course there were still the "whine nights" where he'd go on and on about himself, deprecate others and pump me for information about the family. But now I had nothing to offer, as I had had no contact for so long. Occasionally we'd go out to dinner or I'd volunteer to drive my dad and my stepmom to the airport for their many exciting trips abroad. But even when things were at their best, there was always a sense of distance and formality. When I'd receive post-cards or an occasional birthday greeting from them, he would sign it "Fondly, your Father" or "Fondly" followed by his initials. When Dad would act up or be rude to me or my stepmother, which was frequently, I'd call him on it right away. Sometimes he acknowledged it and would modify his behavior temporarily. As long as I was strong it went all right with him. The bottom line was that Dad didn't like weakness of any kind. Then several things changed.

My divorce started to get complicated. Originally, Richard and I had agreed to a sane and amicable divorce so that legal fees wouldn't eat up our assets. It was a struggle but I paid for everything and handled filing all the paperwork myself. I did not want alimony. Responsibility for each of our bills, bank accounts, credit cards and assets would remain separate, as they had been all along. I only wanted my freedom and the mountain property that was my inheritance from my aunt after my cousin's death.

The problem was that Richard liked the mountain property and wanted it for his own. He wanted out of the city, this was part of the reason we were divorcing, as he had been gone most of the time. After much discussion, we agreed to buy out each other's interests. In order to accomplish this, I had to quitclaim my deed over to him, a tenuous moment where I had to entrust an angry, bitter man with my life and future. But this would allow him to take out a loan to then give me my share from the proceeds.

The other part of the plan was to sell the city house so that he could have the $15,000 equity after the mortgage was paid. But he wanted no part of the necessary steps it would take to accomplish that. It became my part of the deal to fix up the city house and put it on the market. To do that, I had to put thousands of dollars of essential repairs on my credit card at an extremely high rate of interest and carry it for an undetermined length of time. It was also my responsibility to care-take and maintain the house and yard and to deal with the realtors and open houses until the house sold. Six months went by and there had been only one low offer on the house. It was the height of the recession, real estate was tanking, and I was becoming exhausted trying to handle it all.

Richard was becoming impatient with the economy and the delays and speaking with the realtors at every turn to make trivial decisions about this or that. He wanted me to deal with it all. He wanted out and said he would sign a quitclaim to me so that I could make decisions about the sale, one caveat, however, was that I would still be paying *his* loan and *he* would still be getting the credit every time I paid *his* mortgage payment. It was a bad deal, but I had no choice. He also gleefully shared that it was his hope that I'd default on the loan, then he'd have both properties and I'd be out on the street.

So here I was, fresh out of school, in debt up to my eyeballs, starting a business in a bad economy with very little money, paying my husband's mortgage, borrowing furniture to make the house decent to show, plus doing all the yard work myself. To top it off, Richard's creditors now began calling me to pay *his* bills, as he decided to quit his job on advice from his friends who were afraid that I might go after his assets.

At one point I became so overwhelmed I just wanted to quit, let Richard have everything and just walk away with nothing, I just couldn't manage it all. I told my dad I wanted to do this and asked him if I could come and stay with him for a while until I got on my feet.

Without a moment's hesitation he said "NO! There is too much water under the bridge between us and we like our privacy here." I left in stunned silence.

It was like a cold slap in the face of a hysterical person. I went home and had a good cry and quietly decided that I would try my best on my own. I don't know what I had been thinking. Maybe I wanted to see if the closeness I was now feeling toward my dad was real or a figment of my imagination because I wanted a sense of family so much. In retrospect, he actually did me a favor because I became an "adult" that day. I do not fault him for that decision, it would've been disastrous.

I worked until exhaustion every day for months, barely making ends meet. There was no relief in sight. To further complicate things I became ill with pneumonia from all the stress. I felt like I could easily die. It was not a happy time.

Then one day out of the blue, my dad offered to pay off Richard and get him off my back! I guess he saw that I was really toeing the line. I was shocked and surprised, remembering the letter from my 21st birthday where he said I should never ever expect help from him and I never did. He said I could pay him back at the rate of $100 per month until it was paid back. This was very helpful and I was grateful, but it was not money in my pocket. Yes, it was one relief to get my ex off my back, but now this would add an extra $100 burden to my already heavy load. What I really needed was time to get my business established to a point where money was coming in regularly; where I didn't need to supplement the deficit from credit card advances to survive. All I could do now was hope that the emotional respite from Richard's demands might help me cope better with the new financial stress that was added; that, and the fact that the mortgage that I had been paying for all this time could now finally be transferred in my name. I did not want to let my dad down under any circumstances, especially after he had given me this second chance, of sorts. So every month I struggled with the enormous debts and responsibilities of getting work and getting paid in a depressed market. And every month I scraped the $100 together to give my dad, doing without basic necessities many times. I did this for nearly four years.

To help with the burden at several desperate points, I thought it might be helpful to have roommates with whom I could share expenses. In some cases, this proved to be worse than going it alone as they did not or could not pay their share, forcing me to deal with that extra stress and financial burden as well.

One of my roommates, however, proved to be a jovial and happy individual . And despite his poor financial condition, brought much joy to the house. Rob's culinary skills were exemplary, and occasionally he'd test his recipes out on my dad who was always up for an "adventure." He proved to be an effective source of comic relief from the tense formality between my father and me. Unfortunately when he left, things went back to the way they were.

One unanticipated and distressing by-product of this financial transaction was a certain sense of entitlement now displayed by my father regarding access to my home. It seriously forced the issue of boundaries and respect.

GETTING RESPECT

For many years, I was used to being poorly treated. I expected to lose. I hated conflict and confrontation and would avoid them at any cost. The self-deprecating, apologetic behavior I adopted was something I did because I believed everyone else was so much more worthy than I was. As I started to integrate my new healthy behaviors, a natural result was my increasing self-respect. But it would not be so easily won. I would be tested on this, and my very own father would challenge my new understanding and courage to implement it.

When I was a little girl, my father would enter my room without knocking. He'd then scrutinize what I was doing, bark a couple of orders for me to do post haste, and then he'd leave. I hated these intrusions. They always upset me and made me feel off balance. Whatever peace I was able to muster was routinely disturbed, and it didn't matter if I was doing homework or artwork. There was no respect for any of it.

When my father and I tried to renew our relationship on a more adult level, this behavior once again surfaced. But this time there were greater consequences.

Dad would routinely stop by without calling. I could be with a client, working on a project, busy with a phone call or preparing for a meeting. It didn't matter if it was inconvenient for me. Sometimes he would engage my clients in a conversation and say inappropriate things to them like," So you're a bouncy one, aren't you?" "Do you have any education, really?" His capacity for tactlessness always had me on edge. But now we were dealing with my livelihood. Something had to be done. Because he had helped me, I didn't feel I had the right to just come right out and say, "Dad, I need you to call before you come over. Sometimes it's just not convenient and I can't visit with you properly when I am preoccupied with business." He never did take these kinds of things well, and I didn't want to hurt our fragile new relationship. I didn't know what to do. As it turned out, a Higher Power intervened on my behalf.

One day I was working in my office in the back of the house. There was a commotion with sirens and helicopters flying directly over my home. I heard noises behind my office wall and was petrified that the perpetrator had climbed over the fence into my yard. I called the police and was told to lock the door to the office and stay put. I was locked in there for hours, petrified that whoever it was might come to the office where I was.

I don't know if they ever caught the guy who must've jumped the fence to escape, but the incident sufficiently frightened me into action. I decided to install a wrought iron gate for protection. At the time I was a woman alone. It was easy for people to have access to my property and my equipment. Getting a gate was a smart thing to do. Plus, there was an additional perk; Dad could not just routinely stroll in. He would have to make arrangements with me prior to his arrival like everybody else did.

The first time my father encountered the gate, his sour look could've melted the lock. He started to shake it as if trying to will it open. I heard the noise and came out. "What's this?" he asked. I answered, "I was very frightened by an incident the other day. I got this for my protection. You do want your daughter to feel safe, don't you?" "Well, you're going to get a buzzer so I can get in," he said matter-of-factly, with no reference to what I had just asked him. "No, Dad, I'd really prefer it if you'd call first before you come over. I get nervous to be dropped in on suddenly, especially after what happened last week," I countered.

He waved his hand in disgust and left. I did not see Dad for six months after that. He simply would not call me or come over. I felt very bad, but I stood firm. I had to stand firm or my point would never have been made. It was tough for me, because before this I always had backed down when things got uncomfortable. This was very uncomfortable. My father knew the gate was installed for my safety and peace of mind, and yet he would not agree to make a simple phone call to announce his arrival. Eventually he did come by again and he did call first. But it was a very difficult and lengthy roadblock to overcome. I did not wish to be discourteous but I couldn't tolerate the intrusive and disrespectful behavior, regardless who it came from, even if it was my father.

This incident also proved something else to me. I had not been imagining anything. Dad was not naturally inclined to give me the respect I wanted and deserved. I had to demand it and accept nothing less, or it would not be given. I had to fight for it.

From the standpoint of my long-term development, once I was able to stand up to my father, standing up to others became somewhat easier. When unpleasant things would inevitably surface, I learned how to face them head on despite the tremendous discomfort I felt. I eventually became quite fearless in speaking my mind, as I did not want to live with unresolved resentments or lingering problems festering inside. I strove to try and deal with things as they came up.

REALLY NEEDING DADDY'S HELP

Richard could upset me better then anyone I knew. During the course of our relationship, I suffered two miscarriages because there was always so much arguing and contention in the house. By the end of our time together, a single negative word from Richard could cause me so much physical distress that I would feel as though my blood was boiling.

At the end of our relationship, it happened to be time for my routine exam with my OB-GYN, Dr. Matthews. I had known Matthews for over 22 years. I met him when I fell off a horse and was taken to the hospital with a suspected broken jaw. While in X-ray, they discovered that I had been pregnant. Matthews was called in to do a "D and C." I was 19 then, and had not yet figured out what the consequences of sex were. I did not know I was pregnant. Despite the fact that my father was a doctor and my mother a nurse, my parents and I never had "the talk" and I was truly ignorant. After that, Matthews treated every female illness and complaint I ever had, and there were many. He performed an appendectomy on me; he held my hand through my miscarriages and comforted me through my losses. He also spoke to Richard on the proper and kind way to treat me while I was going through all this. Dr. Matthews also performed my tubal ligation when I somberly decided that I couldn't handle another pregnancy. But in retrospect, I believe that deep down I didn't trust myself to be a good parent with what I had been shown about parenting. In short, Dr. Matthews had a warm and kind bedside manner. I liked him and trusted him implicitly.

Several days after my exam, Dr. Matthews called me personally to tell me that he was concerned about some abnormal cells he found in my pap test. His personal call was unusual and it terrified me. Was it the big "C?" I asked tentatively. He answered, "No, it was Pre-C." He said he wanted to monitor me closely and asked me to come in for exams more frequently than once a year. I quickly agreed. But after the fear subsided, financial issues took precedence and because I had no health insurance, I did not come in until I could afford it, which wasn't often.

Once Richard was out of my life though, I began to calm down. And although there were still major financial stressors in my life as a result of our divorce, none of them were as debilitating emotionally as he was. I felt my body and mind improving for a time.

Then one day I felt pregnant. But I knew I couldn't be, because not only had my tubes been tied but I hadn't been with anyone for nearly a year. And unless there was an immaculate conception going on, it simply wasn't possible. I told my father about this and he thought it could be something as serious as diabetes or as benign as a bladder infection. I scheduled an appointment with Dr. Matthews right away.

The doctor told me that I had fibroid tumors, one larger than a grapefruit. He said it wasn't life threatening but that they could be very uncomfortable and could cause heavy, prolonged bleeding and painful irregular periods. The only way to be rid of them was a complete hysterectomy, a myomectomy, or I could simply live with it. I felt ill from the news. I didn't have the resources or the time to recuperate from an operation. I was upset. I needed my dad. He would know what to do. He had resources and pull at many medical facilities, surely his years in medicine could be of help to me now. I called and asked to come over to talk to him.

Once there, I told Dad how upset I was at what Dr. Matthews told me and I asked if there was some way he could help me with an ultrasound test to find out what's going on. Unbelievably he laughingly said, "Now you know what it feels like to carry around a five pound bag of flour in your belly." "What did you say?" I looked at him in utter disbelief. "Now you know what it's like carry around a five pound bag of flour in your belly." He repeated. "Or maybe a full grown cat. Come let's feed the 'little one'."

I felt nauseous from his callous comment and made the conscious effort to compose myself enough to ask him. "Do you think you could help me with an ultrasound test through one of your resources. I don't have health insurance and I can't afford it otherwise" He said he would look into it.

I asked Dad this same question again when we spoke every time for several months, then I stopped asking, figuring he would tell me when it was set up. The set up never came and now it had become a year later. It was time again for my annual check up with Dr. Matthews.

Matthews' demeanor frightened me on this visit. His normal jovial self was nowhere to be found. After the exam, he looked at me and simply said " I want to do a complete hysterectomy on you right away." I was stunned. "Why, what's wrong with me?" I asked. "There are things going on in there that I don't like at all," he responded. I said "Doctor Matthews, you are scaring me badly. I've known you all my adult life and I've never seen you like this. What's scaring me is what you're NOT saying." He said, "I don't want to say anything yet." All I could assume was that it was the worst, the big "C." I was out of my mind by this time.

After the exam, he showed me brochures about the different surgical procedures he was recommending. I looked at all the pamphlets in horror. I DID NOT WANT MY INSIDES REMOVED, and I said so vociferously. "What alternatives do I have?" I asked. He said "OK, to make sure, I want to schedule an ultrasound test so we can really see what's going on. Come in a week from Thursday."

I went home feeling like my life was over. I couldn't believe that I would go through all of this hell to end up dead from cancer. I thought about all the anger, resentment and rage that I had been carrying all my life. It must've been eating away at me all this time. I thought about all the positive work I had done to change my thinking and my life. Wasn't that worth something?

Then I thought of Dad, who never even mentioned getting me help even though I had asked him so many times. This time I did not call him to tell him anything. I didn't need ridicule at this time and I knew I could not count on him for anything else.

Instead I prayed, cried and pleaded with God. I made a deal with myself. If the ultrasound showed any glimmer of hope at all, I promised I would change my life, do something about my eating habits and sedentary lifestyle. I'd take off the extra weight I had put on from stress. I would take care of myself. I would turn the tide. I just needed time.

All that week I struggled with fear and terror at what the doctor would find through the ultrasound test. I didn't sleep or eat well and I spoke to no one.

The day of the test came. I was to drink many glasses of water and was to hold it in until the test was over. I waited for what seemed like an eternity on the uncomfortable lobby sofa. Then I was called in to the examination room. I felt like I was being sent to the gallows. The technician put the cold gel on my belly and proceeded to scan the area. I watched her face intently for some sign of what she was seeing, some telltale hint of what was going on inside of me. I had never felt terror like that before in my whole life. Then it was over. The technician left and I was told to wait for the doctor. When Dr. Matthews came in, I looked in his eyes. I wanted to see if I could read him before he said anything. I held my breath.

Dr. Matthews said deliberately, "You are just a hair's-breadth under critical range with the inflammation in your ovary, but I'm not convinced that I should let you out of here without a hysterectomy…TODAY!" I burst into tears…with relief. He continued, "You're just a few years away from menopause, you wouldn't be losing much. You wouldn't have any more problems with the fibroids either. We could put you on low dose hormone replacement therapy. I'd really like to get you in the operating room today." I didn't even hear what he was saying. All I could focus on was "a hair's-breadth under critical range," thinking "I'll take it!" I'll keep my promise. I'll change my life. Thank you, God. Thank you! I told Dr. Matthews to give me some time and if things didn't improve, he could cut me up all he wanted. He hesitatingly agreed. Then I asked Dr. Matthews, "Look Doctor, how would you feel having your manhood butchered and be given hormones for the rest of your life?" His said, "I see your point." We hugged each other and said goodbye. I felt like a fish that fell off the hook.

I did keep my promise to myself. I changed my diet, eating more fresh fruits and vegetables and less processed foods. I took vitamins and minerals. I started working out, slowly at first, then getting progressively stronger. Within a few short months I lost 30 pounds. I looked better, I felt better, and I had more energy than I ever had before.

I lost more than weight at this time; I also lost respect for my father. I went through the ordeal of a lifetime alone. I couldn't forget that. When

I needed his support, all I got was ridicule. I couldn't forget that. The help he promised was never delivered, never even mentioned. All of these things chipped away at our now deteriorating relationship. I had to come to grips with the fact that it was just like the old days. Nothing had really changed after all. For all intents and purposes I still had no family I could count on.

As the months wore on something else happened, writing the $100 checks to my dad became harder and harder. My hand actually would shake while trying to write them out. This progressively got worse. I started to feel like an Auschwitz survivor paying off Hitler. It felt really bad, but I stayed the course, under no circumstances did I want to let him down.

Chapter 14

The blind shall be made to see – Matt. 11:5

THE LAST PITIFUL STRAW...

Out of the blue, I received a call from my very first boyfriend Barry, back from junior high school 30 years before. He was my very first dance, my very first kiss when I was 15 years old. He was working nearby and happened upon my name in the phone book. He asked if I was who he thought I was, and if so, could he come to see me and get together. I had the fairy tale notion that things like this could happen and change your whole life in an instant. I was excited to see him after all these years. I said yes.

I was disappointed when Barry came by. He had not grown an inch since junior high. I would have to wear flats. I, however, thought I should give it a chance, because overall he wasn't bad looking and he appeared somewhat successful. He thought I had weathered the years well. What he didn't know I wasn't going to share with him. We went out, actually had a good time reminiscing about the past and both of us thought it would be fun to get together again.

On our next date, a party, for some reason we barely spoke. I instead had a stimulating conversation with an interesting couple while he made the rounds with his friends. It felt awkward. But somehow we both agreed to get together again.

It was during our next dinner that he shared with me about the woman he was seeing and how she was not quite challenging enough for him. He referred to himself as Bluebeard and quite a cad toward women. It was at this moment I should've gotten up and left. And although I didn't like the fact that he had a long term someone and was going out with me, I let it slide...because with my convoluted way of thinking I thought maybe I could change him. I thought it was about time that I got a break in the relationship area, and besides, he had traveled 30 years from my past to get here. Maybe it was me that he was looking for.

Barry explained that he was getting ready to dump his girlfriend, opting instead for someone more stimulating and less predictable, someone like me. I guess I was flattered. I shared my notions of soul mates and destiny. He listened politely. Then he shared his claimed expertise with Tantric Yoga. I really should've left. I was so convinced that I was ready for THE ONE and that it should be NOW that I didn't bother to consider if I even liked the little son-of-a-bitch. Turns out I didn't.

The showdown came when I allowed him to talk me into taking it to the "next level." He had made the decision to dump the girlfriend and pursue me exclusively. I told him of my fears about doing this as it might jeopardize our friendship and the good memories we have had about each other for 30 years. He convinced me it was the next step and like an idiot I reluctantly agreed. After all, I reasoned, we had to know if we were compatible in the physical area.

When the day came for our venture to the "next level" I found out the truth. He was no expert in anything after all. Our intimacies felt awkward, forced and uncomfortable. I instantly regretted it. I realized then that I might have known him 30 years ago, but in every way that counts, he was a stranger to me. We were not compatible physically and I wanted to stamp the experience out of my mind and go back to the way it was. But you can't "unring" the bell. At the time I still felt it was impolite to tell him the unpleasant truth, so I improvised acting natural. I couldn't wait to get out of there. The supreme idiocy is that I still believed it could work somehow, despite all the signals to the contrary.

I suppose I wanted emotional support for how weird our encounter made me feel, so I called him the next day. I heard a woman laughing in the background. I asked who that was and he explained that he had second thoughts about dumping the girlfriend after all. I was way too challenging, but perhaps he could have us both…how would that be?

I let him have it. He *had* destroyed our friendship and my sweet memories from junior high. He was right. He was a cad and a scum. He was lower than dog excrement on my shoe. I explained I didn't have people like him in my circle and to please never call me again. He seemed genuinely shocked at my admonishment. But that, as they say, was that.

This scenario in and of itself was no big deal in the scheme of things, but it was another stellar failure in a parade of failures. Plus, something else was happening to me. I was getting tired of this pattern, because I now was beginning to see that it *was* a pattern. I was beginning to get an indescribable restlessness and desire to drastically change things. I was now 45 years old and I was making the same mistakes over and over. It wasn't getting better. I needed to put my foot down and figure out how to stop this pattern. I couldn't go on like this.

READY FOR THE TRUTH

As I meditated about what to do, I got a strong prompting that the answer lay with knowing the truth about my relationship with my father. I called and arranged to see him, telling him only that I was contemplating a change in my career. My goal was to approach this meeting with an open heart and mind, to look with a fresh perspective on the interaction and dynamics between us. As I drove to his house I felt a moment of dread at what I might learn coming from this vantage point.

As always it was one of his wine drinking sessions, but this time it felt different. Inexplicably, I felt it could be the last time we would ever get together like this again. I became acutely aware of every nuance, to see if I could've been wrong about him all these years. Was there love there that I just was not seeing? I had to know for sure.

Father was in particularly good spirits, having imbibed a bit before I arrived. On the table were very old family pictures of my grandma and grandpa. It was particularly bittersweet to see Grandpa's picture. I loved him so much. I sat there as my dad went on and on about his beautiful and charming assistant and how wildly successful she was, and a colleague's daughter and how wildly successful, prominent and wealthy she had become, and himself and how brilliant and successful his career was; I then realized that he didn't even see me. The talk just droned on and on and on. When he got into belittling my brothers, I decided to let him know that perhaps he wasn't the easiest person to please and that it was hard for all us kids to be wildly successful when we were always afraid of being ridiculed and punished. He looked at me squarely in the eye as if he finally understood how difficult it must've been growing up with him and said, "I never abused my kids." I thought it odd and telling that he would go there and it provoked an angry feeling within me. I found myself wanting to scream *OH YES YOU DID…PSYCHOLOGICALLY!!!!* I wanted to tell him about the years of tears and therapy and the heartache and self-hatred and my sometimes-dangerous quest for his approval.

Instead I buttoned it and changed the subject." I think I'm going to be changing careers. "You'll still be in the same business, right?" he asked. "I don't know yet…call it middle age crisis. I need a change and I'm having trouble knowing exactly what to do." I answered. Then he went on and on about a female colleague who was in a similar place in her life and how he helped her into a different field of medicine and was wildly successful n o w. And how he didn't start traveling until he was fifty, and how he didn't earn dime one until he was 30. As he spoke, a lot of negative feelings started to well up inside me. I felt angry and impatient with the same old routine and diatribe. I started to see just how insignificant I was to him as he talked of everything and everyone else. It was becoming abundantly clear that he simply was not capable of loving attention towards me. Self-aggrandizement and cold hard facts were what he was comfortable with.

Sensing my growing discomfort, I did not want an altercation with him so I just dealt with it the best I could and tried to control my breathing. But, if I had the guts I would've told him the truth. *"I DON'T WANT TO SEE YOU ANYMORE. I DON'T WANT TO HEAR YOUR NEGATIVITY ANYMORE. I WILL NOT ACCEPT YOUR DISRESPECT ANYMORE. I DON'T WANT TO CHECK IN WITH YOU SO YOU CAN BELITTLE ME AND CRITICIZE MY EFFORTS. I DON'T WANT TO HAVE TO JUSTIFY MY BELIEF IN GOD TO SOMEONE WHO DOESN'T BELIEVE IN ANYTHING. I NO LONGER CARE IF I HAVE YOUR APPROVAL. YOU ARE A RUDE, TACTLESS, UNLOVING LITTLE MAN THAT I NO LONGER WANT IN MY LIFE…FATHER OR NOT."* Instead I shut up, like I always did, like I was trained to do from childhood. But then I surprised myself by asking him for a temporary reprieve from the $100 a month until further notice. Apparently my soul thought that I needed a complete break from him. Remembering a passage in one of my books, "I will not leave thee lest thou bless me, "I also asked him to bless me on my way regardless of what I decided to do.

Now a bit tipsy, with a mocking papal flourish he waved his hand "I bless you on your way my child." As he did that, I, all of a sudden, felt that this would be the last time I would see him and he was oblivious. It was difficult to see through my flood of tears on my drive home. So this was it! After 45 years. This was all I'd get in the father department. I felt sick. Somehow I managed to finally get home. Once I arrived I went to the backyard and fell to my knees in pain. Such deep sobs came out of me I could barely breathe. The fibroids that had been under control for months at that very moment flared up to such a degree that I was hunched over in pain. I crawled to my bed. I was bleeding profusely. The timing on this manifestation was no coincidence. I had read in my healing books that problems in this area of a woman's body were created by a negative relationship with members of the opposite sex, and that's all I had ever known.

I had been having trouble in this area all my adult life. But now I finally knew the truth. My father, for whatever reason; perhaps because I was a girl, or because I was firstborn, or simply because I was born at all, was not capable of loving me. I now would have to acknowledge it and accept it finally and irrefutably. I would never have the love I needed or wanted from my father. PERIOD. This was part of the physical release of that knowledge. It was part of the healing. I tried not to let it frighten me, but this manifestation was to last for four days.

I would've liked to believe that the information I had acquired from this last interaction cured everything, but it wasn't the case because I hadn't been completely truthful with my father. In order for me to be genuinely free I had to have the guts to tell him the truth. I just couldn't do it face to face. In person he could interrupt me, walk away, belittle me, distract me. He could tune me out.

After two and a half months of deliberation, I gathered my courage and I wrote Dad a truthful letter describing my experience growing up in his care or lack thereof. I came clean about the fact that I had been in counseling for 15 years at the cost of nearly $30,000. Plus, I told him that I would not be able pay him the remaining $10,000 I owed him. Although this went completely against the grain of what I knew to be right and wrong, I felt under these circumstances it would've been wrong to continue to pay. I wrestled with this a long time. I remembered how my parents, during the course of their divorce, saw fit to decimate a $10,000 savings account set up for me by my grandparents. I also came to know that my stepmom had asked father to forgive the debt, reminding him that it had come from Grandma's estate, stating that Grandma had been my first mother and most certainly would've wanted me to have it. No matter how I looked at it, I figured they already had my money. Just to be fair, though, I explained that I would gladly accept a third of the blame for the debt just because I had been born; the $4,800, which I had already paid plus a check for $200 that I was enclosing making it an even $5,000. I explained that he and Mother could shoulder the other two thirds of the debt for the damage they inflicted on my life and me. It was a very matter-of-fact letter, written for a very matter-of-fact man. I'm sure it was a blow.

Just writing it was liberating. I felt a surge of relief and energy I hadn't felt since I was a child. A part of me was cheering loudly just for having the guts to put it on paper. The child in me was cheering her hero…me! This was the first step in finally standing up for myself. But then came Part B, mailing the letter. Did I have the guts to do that?

That letter stayed in my possession for the next 3 days as I sat on the fence about what to do. I struggled. "This would certainly break our relationship." I would counter, "What relationship? It had been nothing but destruction and negativity for 45 years." I questioned, "But what if it got better?" I reasoned, "If it hasn't gotten better in 45 years, what makes you think he will change?" I countered, "But isn't a negative, unloving father better than no father at all?" I whispered, "No, it isn't." Then I had to face the horrible truth. HE WAS NEVER GOING TO CHANGE. I had to remember what I had learned…he simply wasn't capable of being the loving father that I needed. Maybe I'd never know why he couldn't love me, but I had to deal with it and get on with it. I'd be no worse off than I was right now. I drove to the post office and mailed the letter.

Once I came home from the post office, something unexpected happened. After enjoying a brief moment of victory for having the courage to champion myself, I started to become angry. It grew and grew. I was becoming angrier than I had ever been. I never really experienced this feeling before. It scared me. Foul words came spewing out of me. Words that I didn't even know I knew. My cats stared at me with wide eyes, then ran in terror. This wasn't merely anger. THIS WAS RAGE…I never felt anything like this before. It wasn't polite for little girls to be angry. It wasn't spiritual to be unforgiving. But I was angry, enough so for a lifetime. Angry, for the years of ridicule, emotional neglect and alienation. Angry, for the years of emotional torment and anguish. So this is what it felt like to be MAD AS HELL. Now other thoughts began racing in my head "Why did I have to sacrifice my life, put my life on hold because of some unloving egomaniacal manic-depressives, who didn't even believe in getting help for themselves?" I didn't know what to do with myself. I beat, screamed, cursed and sobbed inconsolably until I fell into an exhausted heap on the bed. Then I slept for two days. After that I woke up to a new world, a different world that would be of my creation.

For many months after sending the letter, I hoped my dad would finally understand the negative impact his behavior had on my life. A part of me hoped that he would acknowledge and apologize, father to daughter, so that we could move on to a more truly adult, healthy, relationship. Although it was my hope, I never heard from him again. That was over seven years ago at the time of this writing. He never cashed the check.

On a subsequent Father's Day I sent Dad a small crystal statue reminiscent of a game my brother and I played as children. Brother pretended to be a deadly rhinoceros that could instantly kill Daddy with his poisoned horn. I was the magical unicorn that had the antidote to save Daddy's life. The small crystal unicorn symbolized a little girl's genuine love for her daddy. Through this gift, I wanted him to know that I was okay. That it was all okay. The gift was never acknowledged.

PART 7: CRUCIBLE

Chapter 15

Choose this day whom you will serve – Matt. 6:24

Facilitating the release of my own unhealthy emotions that were stored inside of me was proving to be the key to unlocking the prison doors that had held me captive up until now. All this time I had not been aware that these powerful wardens of anger and fear resided comfortably within me. There were many reasons I couldn't have known that, many reasons why it took so long.

COMING TO TERMS WITH NEGATIVITY

I was brought up to believe that the world outside was bad. That people were bad. I saw my dad carry a gun to work, because he worked in a bad area with a lot of crime. When we went on family vacations, it was always to remote places, "To get away from people." When I went to my first junior high school dance, my dad insisted upon going too, despite the three chaperones we already had, because something bad might happen. By the end of this indoctrination, I was pretty much afraid of the bad world and all the bad people. I couldn't handle the fearsome reality of it.

When I was forced into going out on my own, I had to find a way to live in the world and avoid it at the same time. Drugs and alcohol weren't good enough for masking all of the the terror. To counteract all this doom and gloom, a part of me adopted the belief that if I simply did not acknowledge the ugliness and negativity, or simply refused to look at it or to play the game, it would go away by itself. As long as I didn't examine it too closely, and could keep myself isolated and protected from it, I'd be okay. Of course, life became small indeed. Sometimes it took all the courage I had just to step out of the front door, lest something terrible happened. But eventually, I had to realize that avoiding the truth and being a provisional "pollyanna" was not living.

In order to have a real life, I'd have to really acknowledge some of the truths about life on earth; Sometimes bad things happen, sometimes life hurt, sometimes people hurt other people. Sometimes life was simply unfair. Pain and negativity just a part of the package.

This was a very big and bitter pill for me to swallow. It took me months to digest this one and even try to assimilate it. Eventually, though, I came to see that an important part of the equation had been left out of my education. Sometimes wonderful things happened. Sometimes life was great. Sometimes people were kind for absolutely no reason. I needed to know these things to be able to go on.

When the bad stuff that life could dish out was so bad, all I could do sometimes was to ride it out, pray and hope for the best. At other times, dealing with it was a matter of acknowledgment, an honest appraisal, a change of attitude and/or taking some action. I could do those things. But when it came to other people's negativity, that was another matter altogether.

CONFLICT RESOLUTION

As a child, my father's anger always scared the crap out of me. One day I hid in a closet just to avoid interacting with him. His temper and disagreeable nature upset me so much that it took me sometimes days to recover from one of our encounters. I'd prepare myself days in advance and bolster my courage when I knew I would have to see him. Sometimes I would write myself notes and try to memorize them so I wouldn't appear so frightened and unintelligent in front of him. It never worked. He didn't think much of me. I knew it, and acted accordingly around him as I had been programmed to do. The feeling I had was that he was something and I was less then nothing.

For the most part, father's liberal use of anger proved to be a useful tool in getting everyone in the household to comply with his desires to run a tight ship. It certainly worked. But instead of being a tight ship, it was an unhappy ship. The "Captain Bligh" method of commanding the household just wasn't a healthy, positive way for a family to live on a day-to-day basis. There was a great deal of underlying resentment and hurt that simply was never acknowledged or dealt with in any way. My father never dreamed of hearing any of our grievances. "That, my dear, is your problem," or "Oh, you poor thing," said mockingly, was the extent of his compassion. He didn't believe in apologizing...ever.

I remember seeing a show called "Father Knows Best." It was astonishing to see that "Father" cared about his kids' feelings as well as teaching them life's lessons. He was a dad who could apologize and show that he was human. I never saw anything like that!

When I was about 20-years old, I wanted acknowledgement and an apology from my dad so our relationship could go on. I wrote him a heartfelt letter about how his behavior had adversely affected me. I hoped that if I pled my case successfully, he would realize what he was doing and say he was sorry. We could fix things and have a fresh start. I couldn't have been more wrong. He sent back the letter corrected in red pen like a homework assignment! I was devastated. So much for stating my case. To him I had no case, upper or lower. With him it was either a screamfest or the silent treatment. There was no middle ground.

There was nothing more frightening to me than going up against someone's potential anger. I'd rather run away and avoid any conflict altogether. In my relationships, I found it difficult to voice a grievance or have the courage to address a problem of any kind. Confrontation frightened me so much that I would've rather thrown away the whole relationship than face someone's possible angry return. I couldn't take it, as I thought it would be like my dad's anger. Needless to say, this was very destructive to my relationships. I knew nothing of the true communication and compromise skills necessary to be successful in relating to people, so I'd try to bury and contain the resentment until it eventually would blow. This is how I had seen it done at home. Nobody liked dealing with unpleasant emotions, better to avoid them, sweep them under a rug and hope they'd go away. Of course, the other person didn't know the resentment even existed, then would be shocked by the avalanche of negativity. It wasn't fair at all.

After a few harsh losses brought on by this kind of cowardice, I eventually decided to try a more courageous and positive approach and go the opposite way. If I saw a potential problem or something upset me, I would bring it up instead of burying it. I would be honest and let the person know right up front how things were affecting me, reasoning that if they knew and loved me we could work it out together.

At first, this approach was quite daunting and took everything I had. Inside, I'd be trembling and quailing in fear. Up until then, nobody cared how I felt. Now I was asking someone to listen to me and care about my feelings and respect me. It was a very big step. Many times, however, instead of finding angry responses, I found a willingness to listen and resolve the issue, sometimes not.

After my first tenuous baby steps, I became rather adept at assessing my feelings in a relationship and developing the ability to articulate them successfully and respectfully to the other party. Sometimes it would lead to an argument, which was my worst fear. But time after time I was seeing that no matter how uncomfortable it got, I was coming through it intact. I was beginning to learn how to weather disagreements more successfully. I wasn't as destroyed as I thought I would be. I was learning how to ask for consideration and respect, and get it, or forget it.

At other times speaking up did lead to the final altercation and inevitable breakup that I feared so much. I dealt with that, if and when it would come. Sometimes, instead, it made the relationship stronger. Knowing that I could speak up when necessary, defend myself when necessary, and break up when necessary, gave me a lot more confidence in myself and my ability to have a loving, strong and respectful relationship with someone.

There were certain modes of behavior I found that consistently worked. I would always let a person know if I was upset with them and why. If I had to tell someone that I was angry with them, I would tell them in a calm manner, no yelling, slamming, throwing or hitting. I would never pull the silent treatment. No personal attacks or insults. I would voice resentments as soon as I became aware of them myself. No matter how ugly the return response, I would never return it in kind. I would remain as respectful to the other person as I could. If that were not possible, I would remove myself from the situation as soon as I was able. No vengeful retaliation. Let it go, regroup and move on. Sometimes implementing these behaviors was a most difficult thing to do. But even so, they never added fuel to the fire and I could live with that.

Learning how to stand up for myself and fight fair without running away, was by far one of the most useful and positive relationship tools I have acquired to date.

THE FORBIDDEN EMOTION

Displays of anger by the children in our household were simply not tolerated. It was as though expression of that emotion was a privilege allowed only to the adults, as evidenced by my dad's frequent quote, "Children should be seen and not heard."

Because I was never allowed to vent the hurt and angry feelings I felt to anyone in a healthy way, I learned to stifle it, bury it, turn it inward onto myself. There was simply no other outlet for such powerful feelings. Containing my hurt was a full time job. Neither parent seemed comfortable with negative emotions, other than their own. If I did have a hurt or angry moment that was inadvertently expressed, it was turned back on me and either discounted, mocked, ignored or was grounds for punishment. To survive, I adopted the only behavior that appeared to be acceptable…a false brightness. If I pretended to be okay around them, it seemed to cause them less distress and presented less potential for retribution. So that's what I did, because it wasn't safe to be honest. Unfortunately though, eventually I started to believe those lies myself.

Once when I was perhaps nine years old, my dad decided he should take me to a play. I wasn't feeling well and didn't want to go. I told him so. His reply, "You don't know what sick is, I deal with really sick people all day long." I was burning with fever and had a very sore throat, but he decided we should go anyway. After all, he surmised I might've been faking. I didn't want to ruin his evening and I tried to politely sit there through the show. But I felt faint and needed to tell him so. Dad was obviously perturbed at the inconvenience I had created and angrily took me to his clinic to check me out. There, he discovered I had a temperature of 104 degrees and that I indeed was ill. I felt bad for days because of the inconvenience I had caused him and he let me.

There were also times when I had become an inconvenience to my mother as well. Occasionally after school, long after the last child eagerly climbed into the parent's waiting vehicle, I'd be left there alone and vulnerable on the school steps. I'd be the only kid waiting often an hour or more, to be picked up by a mother who'd gotten otherwise involved shopping for furniture or who had simply forgotten that I was there.
When she did finally show, she'd be quite cheerful and unapologetic, oblivious to my obvious distress. On several occasions, during these lengthy waiting periods, I'd be approached by suspicious or lascivious characters whose lecherous advances involved offers of a ride home…or worse. It was frightening. Sometimes I wondered if she'd ever come for me or if I'd be left there forever.

Incidents like this were plentiful and by the end of my familial tour of duty at age 18, I was a mass of buried resentments, hurt and anger, only I didn't know it yet. Dangerous feelings like this had to come out in one form or another, and they did. I was subconsciously angry all the time, at all the wrong people, especially myself.

Not having anyone to ever hear me out made it all the worse; made me feel like I had to deal with this enormous burden alone. It was my problem. Dad told me so, many times. I thought that's just the way it was supposed to be, and I didn't have the skills to know how to uncover and heal this kind of damage.

Oddly enough I believed I contained it well, what with all my years of training. I thought life was just supposed to feel bad and that the daily gut-grinding discomfort was just part of the deal. During the course of our divorce Richard once said, "You are the most emotionally stunted, angry person I have ever met." I was surprised; I thought I was doing pretty well, considering.

One day, I called a woman's support group for help and the first thing the counselor asked me was "Have you experienced your own rage yet?" I explained that I didn't get mad and that it took a lot to push me over the edge. She laughed. "I'm a spiritual person," I explained, "I don't believe in being angry, I believe in forgiveness and I've forgiven my parents." She said flatly, "Uh-huh."

What I had actually been doing was putting the cart before the horse. Trying to put on the bandage of forgiveness without cleaning out the wound of hurt. It was like putting a band-aid on a broken leg, and it clearly was not working.

The truth was that my own anger scared me. I really had no idea what would be unleashed if I just let go. I felt I had to keep a lid on these feelings because it was safer that way...for everybody. But carrying this kind of baggage around wasn't spiritually uplifting. No matter what kind of forgiveness technique I could muster, the problem was still there; firmly entrenched deep inside me, and would remain there until I had the courage to tap into it and allow myself to "re-feel" the pain and anger. Until I did that, nothing would ever change.

The momentary feeling of triumph after I sent my "truth about me" letter to my dad, almost immediately gave way to the forces of building anger within me. The dam finally had to burst. Things had gone too far for too long and now I had no choice but to let the angry tirade spill out in all its glory. I had lost control of it. I had lost control of myself. The deep inner reservoir of pain was being tapped and the negative and destructive energies that had been building for a lifetime could now finally be released. All I could do was to let it pour out of me and get out of its way until it was done. So there it was. What I had been trying to contain and hide and manage all this time, the dark feelings that were the source of my self-hatred and inappropriate anger to others. This was the vile poison that was consuming me and eating up my life.

Every insult and cruelty that I swallowed as a little girl, every harsh and thoughtless word and action against me could now be expelled. That I was capable of such strong and violent feelings truly shocked and surprised me. I would not like to have met me in a dark alley at this time.

This rage also encompassed something else; the wasted years of my precious life, h aving to sort out somebody else's garbage that had been literally forced on me. What right did they have to push their thoughtless, dysfunctional bilge on me, then blame me for not being what they wanted? They had a moral obligation, especially as parents, to foster their child's growth, not hinder it! Wasn't life difficult enough without this heavy millstone to deal with on top of it? I wanted my 20 years back! The anger I felt was justified towards their cowardly non-action, spiritually lazy, harmful behavior that was left for me to figure out and clean up. WAS I ANGRY? YOU BET I WAS.

I chewed on this righteous anger for many months. Then one day it began to subside, as I realized that they, too, were victims of this very behavior, the emotional, "passing of the buck" mentality that they mindlessly and automatically handed to me. It was the family tradition of trauma and misery. It wasn't personal. Anyone unlucky enough to be born in my position would've gotten the same treatment. It just happened to be me.

I would never forget all that had transpired, but by allowing myself to express my deep seated rage I could now create a change in how I was feeling and reacting to it from this point on. There was a calmer demeanor about me. I didn't have the incessant inner turmoil constantly churning within me. Now that I knew where it had been coming from, I no longer found myself inappropriately angry at others. Astoundingly, venting my anger kicked me free of the vortex of despair and freed me to really live.

As I became more familiar with the reality of the emotion of anger, I eventually came to understand it and respect it as a most important one that needed immediate acknowledgement, conscientious expression and non-destructive outletting, not sublimation.

FORGIVENESS

Without purging the angry, resentful and fearful feelings that I had been carrying, I could not really begin the work of true forgiveness in any form. Afterward, the best I could do for a long time was a healthy indifference towards my parents. Neither love nor hate. I'd had to leave the forgiveness to a Higher Power because I had work to do now. I had a life to rebuild and focus on, and frankly, sorting out their issues had taken up enough of my precious time. I had put my life on hold long enough. They made their choices and now had to live with the consequences, as did I. Now, though, I felt that I actually did have choices, choices that I could finally make for my life on a conscious level.

The most wonderful by-product of the whole experience was that now I could understand and truly forgive myself and feel compassion for the little girl who wanted love and kindness so much. It wasn't hard for me to forgive her past mistakes and want the best for her.

I once saw a billboard that read "The Best Revenge Is To Live Well." I liked that a lot and I adopted that philosophy for myself.

DREAMS OF THE CHILD

After the emotional turbulence of the letter and its aftermath subsided, I began to get vivid dreams of a little girl. She was opening ancient, huge and heavy wooden doors. Her small frame was standing in the dark doorway taking in the beauty of the green and lush outside world that she had not seen in a very long time. She notices the figure of a woman walking down a path and calls to her. She suddenly leaves her dark prison and starts running joyfully towards the woman, who now is aware of the c h i l d 's presence. The woman turns to look and she begins to visibly recognize the child as she approaches. She kneels to be at the child's level and as they meet, they embrace tightly and emotionally.

Eventually the dream reveals that I was the woman embracing myself as a child. It was the spiritual reunion of precious parts of myself that been splintered and separated for too long. I was being restored to wholeness. This dream showed me that I had done the correct, if not difficult thing, in separating from my parents.

Somewhere along my journey, I had read about an exercise to connect to one's inner child. It was suggested to just let go and write whatever came to mind with your non-dominant hand. I decided to try it.

This letter came from that exercise:

Dear Big Alyson,

Thank you for not leaving me behind. Thank you for coming back for me. I love you very much.

Little Alyson

Dear Little Alyson,

I love you so much. I could never leave you. You are very important to me. I'm glad you were born. I'm glad you're a girl. You have all the time in the world to be yourself and get your needs met. You're wonderful.

Big Alyson

Chapter 16

According to your faith be it unto you – Matt. 9:29

RELATIONSHIPS

*I*n truth, I have made every stupid relationship mistake a human being could possibly think of making, and then some. To say that relationships were challenging would be the understatement of my lifetime. I've run the gamut. I've chosen unwisely, I've chosen out of fear; to some I have been closed off, to others I've been too open. I've run away too quickly, with others I stayed too long. Yet despite never having experienced anything remotely close to a healthy relationship, I never gave up. I kept trying and continued learning something precious about myself, and the true nature of love with each and every one. These became my stepping stones to a greater understanding of love.

Had I known the true scope of the enormous emotional work I had to do on myself, I probably never would've gotten involved with anyone. But in my ignorance, and with my desperate need for love, I braved the inevitable heartbreaks to try to find my mate. Like a child outgrows hand-me-downs, so I outgrew relationships. I learned something valuable from each one, things I should've actually have learned as a growing child, but couldn't. I had to start somewhere.

With each came a certain joy and the inevitable heartbreak as I tried to piece together the necessary ingredients to hopefully, one day, finally get it right.

For many years the patterns of failure remained the same, the disappointments predictable. Truthfully, there couldn't have been any other outcome because I was so deathly terrified to really open up to anyone, fearing that they'd be like my father. The "Don't ever let them see the real you or you will die" promise that got me through the "war" of childhood intact, was now turning out to be extremely detrimental to me. But I really didn't know how to be any other way. This had become my standard of operation for my whole life.

Although I couldn't see it at the time, as apparently different as each man seemed to be, they all shared similar characteristics. Each reflected a certain unavailability, similar to that of my father; several through alcohol addiction which was hidden or diminished while courting, some through physical or medical limitations, others through a lack of emotional maturity. All, however, were intelligent and very good at what they did.

My submerged and continuing pain from my father's treatment of me subconsciously drew these relationships to me. I got what deep down I believed I should get, it's what was familiar to me, even though it was unhealthy and made me unhappy. I didn't have the understanding to free myself from the inexorable bonds caused by my sublimated anger and resentment to prevent it from happening again and again. I now have come to believe that choosing these individuals was my attempt to fix the original relationship with my dad in some way. Of course I really couldn't do that through a surrogate, for a true healing I had to go to the source. Nothing less would do.

Eventually it had become clear. The relationship with the first man in my life, my dad, had been disastrous. That had been the unstable foundation on which every subsequent disaster was built. My relating skills acquired through that relationship could do nothing but insure a string of m i s e rable failures and there could be no other outcome. Failure had been my charted course, from which I could never steer clear until I could gain my freedom from it and see it from an unemotional and objective viewpoint. I had this insight during that last face-to-face meeting with my dad, and only when I was ready to know the truth and stop deluding myself. Now the real work could begin.

LEARNING HOW TO RELATE

After I had broken free of my dad's influence over my life, I now had a real dilemma to contend with. I realized that I simply knew nothing about having a healthy relationship. Up until now, all I had been was a superbly successful mimic of my parents' dysfunctional behavior. I had to find another way. I needed the right tools.

I did some research and found a local 12-week relationship support group offered by a licensed family therapist and couples counselor. I signed up and made a commitment to myself to see it through completely.

The first, most astounding thing I noticed about the eight people in the group, was that they all came from similarly unloving backgrounds as I did! This couldn't have been a coincidence. I brought my observation up to the facilitator and the group. He confirmed that this was true of all the attendees he ever counseled. What I was learning was that our input affects the outcome; change the input, most certainly change the outcome. I was more determined then ever to change things for myself.

The first thing I wanted was a clear definition of what love was. I didn't know. I found the answer in a book by Dr. Susan Forward called *Toxic Parents*. She described love this way. "Loving behavior doesn't grind you down, keep you off balance, or create feelings of self-hatred. Love doesn't hurt, it feels good. Loving behavior nourishes your emotional well being. When someone is being loving to you, you feel accepted, cared for, valued and respected. Genuine love creates feelings of warmth, pleasure, safety, stability and inner peace."

This simple paragraph made a big impact on me. I had never experienced anything even remotely close to that description in my whole life. But it became something to strive for. I typed it out and carried this paragraph with me in my wallet, reading it over and over every day. I shared it with the group who all agreed that this was a great definition and they chose to adopt it too.

As "luck" would have it, some friends invited me to a singles' party where I met a nice man. His appearance in my life provided me with the perfect "practice" relationship to work on as I went through 12 weeks of the class. This was the first "icebreaker" relationship since the split with my father. So I was nervous and I wanted to get it right.

Now that I was beginning to value myself and actually cared about what happened to me, I was becoming extremely uncomfortable with even thinking about the dating fast track; the "sex for dinner" scenario. I didn't want any sexual pressure or innuendos of any kind. Despite my chronological age and my prior relationship experiences, for all intents and purposes I was a beginner. I wanted to get to know somebody slowly, to see if we were compatible and had things in common before getting physical too quickly.

I was so uncomfortable with the thought of "wrestling an octopus" after the date that I felt compelled to create my own dating tool of sorts. I wanted something that would protect me, as well as explain where I was coming from so that no one would be misled. I came up with *The Dating Alternative Manifesto*, a "training wheels" tool for a beginning dater like myself. This is what it said:

THE DATING ALTERNATIVE MANIFESTO & CONTRACTUAL AGREEMENT

PART 1
THE PROBLEM

It's impossible to know everything about a person that you need to know from one or two dates. One's prior experiences really have no bearing in the present, because we've gone through these experiences, been changed by them and hopefully have grown in the process. Past behaviors and mistakes can't really apply in this new set of circumstances. Also, limited time because of busy schedules precludes the prolonged interaction required to make sensible decisions about a person's qualities. Second-guessing without all the facts is impractical and might be wrong, thereby excluding a potentially positive connection.

Question: *How do we really know the exact combination of traits that are truly best for us? How many people have made specific lists just to find themselves pleasantly surprised by someone they might never even have considered?*

THE GOAL

To experience the affection, loving attention and acceptance necessary to live a healthy, balanced life; to take the frustrating edge off the physical and emotional deprivation one experiences as a single; to then be free to clearly focus on other matters; i.e. life partner, life work, etc.

TO FACILITATE

(Once, of course, a suitable candidate manifests) To accept each other unconditionally, act lovingly and affectionately toward one another for a mutually set period of time (suggestion - 2 months). For this period of time, assume the best about one another until proven otherwise, trust each other until proven otherwise. Relax, be yourself and be honest without fear of rejection. Communicate freely.

The affectionate behavior can include but is not limited to, hand holding, kissing, hugging, embracing, friendly sharing and confiding, no intercourse. This is to allow time to get to know each other unencumbered by the emotional complications of physical intimacy. (The specifics should be worked out to what is comfortable with the parties involved.)

At the end of the set period, the terms of the contract can be renegotiated or terminated without major trauma to either party, perhaps establishing a friend or more for life in the process.

This agreement shall be rendered immediately null and void should intolerable or unacceptable behavior surface at any time during the trial period.

❑ *Yes, I understand the concept! OK, I'll give it a shot for 2 months.*

_____ Date _____
_____ Date _____

PART 2
QUICKIE SOCIAL COMPATIBILITY CHECKLIST
List recreational outings/functions you've attended in the past year and see if your partner would have liked to have gone or not.
(Rate on a scale of 1-10)

1) Comedy Club   ____
2) Dance Show   ____
3) Theatrical Play   ____
4) Music Concert   ____
5) Movie   ____
6) Golf/Sports   ____
7) Day Hike   ____
8) Picnic   ____
9) Art Gallery   ____
10) Dress Up Event   ____
11) Party   ____
12) Ask your partner what they have done in the past year and see how it rates with you.

_____

_____

_____

_____

_____

MATT THE GUINEA PIG

I showed this document to my girl friends and I lightheartedly presented it at the singles' party fully expecting to be ridiculed and avoided by the men in the crowd. Instead, I found many people thought it made sense and wanted copies. Matt was one of them. Instead of being turned off by it, *The Dating Alternative Manifesto* proved to be a wonderful conversation starter and the *Quickie Compatibility Checklist* allowed us a fun and casual way to see if we'd make good activity buddies.

When I asked if he was attached in any way, Matt told me that he was divorced and I was glad to hear that. We hit it off right away. In a short time, through the *Checklist*, I learned that we both liked dancing, day hikes, theatre, movies and golf. It was a great place to start.

He called that same evening saying he had such a wonderful time and that he wanted me to come meet him at his office for lunch to "make sure I was real." He was afraid, as I was, that the excitement of the moment produced some unfortunate illusions about each other. However, once we saw each other again, all apprehension vanished, we both liked what we saw in the light of day.

Our first date was a day hike and a short drive through the coastal canyons to the beach. We had a great time and spent the next few weeks faxing and phoning each other with clever and loving messages during the week and going out on weekends. It was harmless adolescent fun. Matt was an extremely outgoing and affectionate person. He did not seem to have any problem opening up and was not afraid of loving or the possibility of being hurt like I was. He drew me out of my shell with his confident easy manner.

Things were progressing and I was beginning to trust him more and more through his encouragement and acceptance. Up until now all we had were some intense make-out sessions, but it was becoming clear that the next physical step was just around the corner.

I felt hesitant. We were only three weeks into the agreement and were already contemplating breaking *The Dating Manifesto* rules. This was a really big step for me. And while I was beginning to have feelings for Matt, a part of me wanted to run away and hide.

Every baby step forward that I took filled me with fear and trepidation about being hurt. Many days I needed time away from it to process it. What seemed so easy for him proved to be tortuous for me. After our dates and interactions, I found I needed to discuss my feelings and fears with my relationship group, who gave me the courage and advice to go on despite my fears. They all, at this point, were living vicariously through me, as I was the only one in the group brave enough to go for it.

Matt had been loved; he knew love, and was loving as a result. I had never been loved and was just learning how to open myself up to it, despite the terror of being hurt. With every hesitant, hard-won step I took, I felt like I fell back three emotionally. I didn't realize that loving someone could feel so bad. I felt very inept at this whole process. Many times I did not want to proceed with the relationship; I did not like the feelings that accompanied what should've been a most joyful part of my life.

In retrospect, it wasn't really loving someone that felt bad, it was the "emotional surgery" to open an area that had been completely shut down for most of my life that felt bad. I was "cleaning the pipes," so to speak. A life force was now being restored to an atrophied and undeveloped part of the loving nature within me, and as uncomfortable as it felt, I instinctively decided to let it run its course and stay out of my own way as best as possible.

Intimate physical expression of our feelings for one another brought about yet more distress to me as it now increased my emotional risk ten fold. It did not make things better for me. It made me feel more vulnerable and fearful.

Shortly after this, the axe fell. It came out that Matt, though separated for over two years, was not actually completely divorced from his 22-year marriage. When I asked him how long before it was over, he confessed that they hadn't even begun the process. I was devastated by the news, and asked why he lied to me and why had he been at a "singles'" party in the first place. He said that neither of them had been in a hurry and that it had been an amicable split because of their child. He explained that he was invited to the singles' party by his friends and saw no harm in it, but he did not expect to fall in love with someone. Now the delay in handling their divorce would be causing a complication in all our lives. I did not like being in this position at all and had I known the truth I would never have allowed myself to get involved with him in the first place. Now it was too late, I was already emotionally invested.

He assured me that it would not be the problem I imagined. He and his ex-wife were friendly towards each other and he didn't see it being a problem at all. His reassurance calmed me down and I trusted him to handle it quickly as he said he would.

In the meantime, Matt was eager for me to meet his ten year old child. This was a scary moment. Anyone who says the opinion of the child of the person you're dating isn't important is a liar. They can make you or break you. Period.

In this case I needn't have worried, as it was love at first sight. Cathy was a sweet and good-natured little girl. Matt was amazed and thrilled at how well we got along and soon we were all going on outings together. It was tremendous fun and I couldn't believe how lucky I was to have two such wonderful people in my life.

As I had no family with whom I could share my news, I wrote a letter to Twilah describing my new relationship. I was so happy and I wanted her to share in my joy.

When I realized that it had been a couple of weeks since I sent the letter, I called Twilah to ask her if she had received it. Her reaction surprised me. She was not happy about anything other than my relationship with Cathy. She came right out and said "This man is not who you think he is, he is just a 'transitional.' Do not put too much stock in him, he is just a bridge." I was furious and upset. How could she say such things, she didn't even know him and I told her so. She said, "I'm sorry, I can't lie to you, this is what I see." I was crushed.

Tearfully, I broke the news to Matt, who did not take it well. He wanted to call her up and tell her a thing or two. He said she obviously didn't know him too well. He told me he loved me, that I was his raison d'etre, and that we didn't need anyone telling us how our future was going to play out, simple as that. It didn't matter anyway.

But deep down it did matter...to me. Twilah's remarks made me have second thoughts about everything. I had really made progress opening up emotionally, I felt happy and secure with Matt and Cathy, but not having her blessing felt really bad. I had many sleepless nights about it because I really trusted this woman.

I was angry with Twilah for putting this burden of unpleasantness on me. "Who is she, to tell me the outcome of my life and my relationships? Didn't I have any say in the matter?" I questioned. The more I thought about it, the more anxious and upset I became and I found that I was contemplating an unbelievable decision. Had it become time for me to say goodbye to Twilah, my surrogate Mom, my healer, my therapist, and my friend of the last 15 years? This couldn't be... and over a guy, no less!

It was all I could think about. Around Matt I pretended that it was all right and that what Twilah said didn't matter, just like he said. But it was becoming increasingly difficult to conceal my unhappiness. I remained on the fence for a few days going back and forth in my mind. If I believed Twilah, what should I do...dump Matt? What if she's wrong? I would never forgive her. And what if I dump Twilah? If she's right and he is transitional...I'd have to handle it alone because I wouldn't have her to run to! Both scenarios were horrible. Why couldn't she just be happy for me and let it go at that?

Then one day I mustered the courage to take action. I called up Twilah and told her that I thought our relationship had gone about as far as it could. I thought it best that we say goodbye. She was very shocked and surprised to hear what I was saying; so was I. She said she was sorry but couldn't lie about what she knew. I told her I understood. I thanked her, told her I loved her and blessed her for all she had done for me. She also blessed me on my way.

With that one call, a fifteen-year relationship with the one person who had been there for me through thick and thin came to a quiet and uneventful end. I sat in stunned silence for a long time. Now it hit me. I was really on my own and I'd have to handle whatever happened alone, as my safety net was gone.

After a period of mourning my loss of Twilah, I decided to give my all to the relationship with Matt and Cathy that now had become my focus. I honestly did the emotional work to dig deep past my discomfort and take the risk to open my heart fully to what lay before me. It was the first time in my life that I had done so in earnest.

I wish I could say that we had a happy ending, but regrettably it was just as Twilah had predicted. Matt found that when it actually came time to finalize things, his soon-to-be-ex was not as agreeable as she had been previously. There were property issues, financial issues, tax issues and, surprisingly, even child custody issues. The divorce became a monster.

One day I saw an odd and far away look in his eyes of the mesmerizing terror that was looming immediately in front of him. He couldn't see past it or how he could possibly sustain his part of our relationship. I offered to lie low and to help him out as unobtrusively as possible in any way I could. After all, I had made a commitment to him and I was going to honor it. But his fear over the situation overtook him, and he felt he had no other choice but to let me go. He assured me that he felt horrible and wanted to make sure that I knew that this sad end was not his original intent in any way. Of course I knew that, but it didn't make it hurt any less. I did not get to say goodbye to Cathy. My heart was thoroughly and completely broken. And now I didn't even have Twilah to help me through it.

At first I didn't believe it. This couldn't be happening. I really thought that at any moment he would find a way for us to make it through. I cried, I prayed, I painted the living room, and then I cried some more. It was not only the distress of losing Matt, but Cathy, who had become so dear to me, was now gone too. The loss was too great. I was extremely depressed and found it difficult to function.

After the breakup, a particularly disturbing nightmare also frequently surfaced. This was the scenario: I would be lying, seemingly dead and desiccated in a tomb. The heavy sarcophagus lid would be moved aside and the scorching sunlight would sear into my mummified flesh, reducing me to ashes as I became consciously aware of all that was happening to me in that one final screaming moment.

I was like a zombie. I did not go out, I hardly spoke to anyone for two months. I thought the pain would never end and I gave serious thought to becoming a nun and living within the safety and protection of a cloistered existence. This had become my life. Then one day a miracle. There was a call on the answering machine, from Cathy! Her little voice saying I miss you and I think about you a lot, do you ever think about me?

It was like I could breathe again. This sweet, loving little creature, pulled the knife out of my heart and stopped the bleeding with a single call. She had taken the initiative to find my number in her dad's phone book and call me. I was so moved I could hardly speak. After I managed to compose myself I called her back. Her dad answered and was shocked when I asked to speak to Cathy. She joyfully came to the phone and as we talked, we reaffirmed our mutual bond of affection, which has lasted to this day.

Matt and I never got back together. After his divorce was finalized he said he regretted his decision to let me go and hinted that he was ready for me now. Occasionally when we'd all get together for dinner I got the feeling that Cathy would've liked to see us get back together. But I had grown up too much for that by then. The real emotional connection with

Cathy has remained an enduring and positive relationship acknowledged for its authenticity and durability by both of her parents. She is still a joy in my life and it was worth everything I went though to have this blessing in my life.

After the debacle with Matt, I did not want to go out ever again. It was simply too painful and I couldn't take it. I thought that I could learn to be content with being single for the remainder of my life. Of course it would be a cowardly thing to do, but most assuredly it would be safe. The more courageous thing to do would be to try again should the opportunity arise. I had survived the worst that could happen to a person as a result of a failed relationship, I survived a broken heart, and somehow I was still alive. Knowing that I could survive the pain of a loss like I did actually did help me make the decision to go forward afresh. Did I want more of that kind of pain? NO! But at least I was armed with the knowledge that I could survive it. That was a great thing to know.

WE MOVE ON

The next person I was to meet did not turn out to be the love of my life. Although at first we briefly toyed with the possibility of a romance because it was once again a singles' party, Hank and I never had a romantic liaison. We shared many common interests and were there for each other when we each needed a shoulder to cry on. In the long term he has proven to be a friend for life, and I would've missed out on that if I had shut myself down.

To cope with my loneliness, however, I had become a workaholic, hiding behind heavy work schedules and impossible deadlines. Fun and relaxation were not words in my vocabulary any longer, and I was actually beginning to worry about myself. I was basically through with the singles' party option forever. But I wanted to find someone to do things with so I next tried the personals. After screening a few unacceptable and quite obnoxious potentials, I agreed to meet with Ethan.

Ethan was not an unattractive man, but there were certain things about him that bothered me. He had been married numerous times, he had six children, he seemed preoccupied with innuendo regarding his sexual discipline and prowess and thought it a good idea to discuss such things way too early in our relationship. He was completely enamored with his own intelligence and he fancied himself a great writer. Every day he would e-mail me enlightening and thought-provoking snippets from great thinkers and authors that he had collected over the years.

At first it was flattering to have such an obviously intelligent and well-to-do gentleman take such an interest in me. But as the weeks progressed I noticed one bothersome thing. Nothing that he ever sent me was original. I was wondering if he actually was capable of a single genuine thought.

One day he sent me a series of poignant questions originally composed by an anonymous writer from another century. I know he believed that they would elicit admiration about his depth of character. Instead it made me mad at his lack of originality. I started to get the feeling that this e-mail bombardment was his standard courting approach, just a lot of smoke and mirrors for gullible and lonely women. I wasn't buying it; it felt contrived. Just for the hell of it, though, I thought I'd actually take the time to thoughtfully respond to each and every question and send it back to him.This is what I came up with. I wish I had kept the original questions.

MY RESPONSE TO ETHAN

What do I ache for?
My counterpart...My Divine Selection.
The One whose life plan meshes seamlessly with mine.
Nothing less will do.

I persist in dreaming and trusting that I will receive what I desire...
When I am ready to receive it.

I will be patience itself. I will perfect myself in preparation to receive.

Indeed, I would risk appearing the fool for love.
What the sleepwalkers of this world think of me is of little importance.

I've experienced sorrow, my own and others,
Felt pain so soul-searing and deep that it crumpled me like paper,
Making conscious breathing the chore of the moment...
Yet I continue to open.

I've known moments of joy and ecstasy,
I need to know more.

I feel no limitations...
The sky is too low.

Despite betrayal,
I still can trust and be trusted.
I would not betray myself to match the actions of others.

I see beauty most everywhere,
And if it is not there, I will create it myself.

I've known failure, and gained something of benefit from the doing,
Success is the mystery yet to be revealed.

God is my source and supply.
If offered vast riches and eternal life to renounce my belief,
I'd choose to die in poverty.

I truly like my company,
If courage, loyalty, resourcefulness, endurance and humor
Were of paramount importance, I'd have me in my foxhole
in an instant.

I'd walk through fire, walk on water,
Dig under, climb over, breakthrough, break free,
Give all I had or do without.

All this would I do and more...
For the ones I love.

Ethan's original one-word response was, "Wow!" Although I liked him, I did not feel a deep connection with Ethan. It might've gone farther but something extraordinary happened instead, something that really caught my attention.

FULL CIRCLE

One day I received a call on my answering machine from a man I had known nearly 25 years before, when he was just 18 and I was 21. Jay and I met and fell in love on a dangerous and exciting high seas adventure on a 57' sail boat. We went through a hurricane, the loss of our sails and engine, a leak in the hull, navigational sabotage, and various personality conflicts from the others on board. Eventually I was to become his "first mate." We went through an extraordinary experience and learned a lot about each other during that time.

When we came back from the trip, our bond of trust was great and we wanted to continue our friendship but were separated by his parents who were overprotective, devoutly religious and didn't approve of me. To get away from them, he enlisted into the Navy and though we wrote occasionally, we eventually lost touch with each other over the years. I had gotten married and moved out of the area.

After he got out of the service, Jay searched for me and was told by a jealous and spiteful ex-boyfriend of mine that I was dead. He mourned for a period of time and then was encouraged to get on with his life. He married a woman who loved him but whom he did not.

After 17 tumultuous and unhappy years together, he finally separated from her. They were described as Nitro and Glycerin. It was at this point that his best friend mentioned it might be a good time to revisit whether or not I was really dead. He searched and, much to his surprise, found me on the internet.

As we reminisced on the phone, the years seemed to melt away and we decided to have a reunion of sorts. Once Jay and I actually saw each other again, the old feelings came flooding back. This would have been wonderful except for one little thing…he was in the beginning stages of what would turn out to be a bitter divorce and there were children involved. It seemed that this scenario was becoming a little too familiar and my first inclination was to run like hell, especially after what I had been through with Matt. But Jay was very persistent.

I've always thought that there's nothing more persuasive then a courting man, and Jay was no exception. Despite my better judgment, I agreed to continue to see him. I said goodbye to Ethan.

For a while things were better then great. His parents, once my bitter adversaries, now embraced me. His coworkers were complimentary as to the positive changes in him since our reunion. Even his neighbors were pleased about the situation. There was so much support for us that it just felt right to proceed. Despite the supportive talk, I still felt very insecure about being in the picture at this particular point in time in his life. This wasn't good timing at all.

But the love-seeking romantic in me was thinking that this was different—it had to be fate. I was thinking that this was the most romantic story that I ever heard and I was in it! It was like a story from a novel. But not all love stories have happy endings. The novelty of our reunion began to fade quickly as the grim reality of things began to surface. I was becoming emotionally invested and I had become a sympathetic ear to his mounting problems. His family and friends, quite simply, were getting burned out with hearing about them.

Then my life changed by one simple allowance. I let Jay bring his computer over to my house so he could stay and work in peace over a holiday weekend. The problem turned out to be that he never left. And I, believing his resurfacing in my life was my destiny, reverted to my cowardly former behavior and did and said nothing to change it. After that, his divorce issues started to escalate. The next thing I knew my home became a battlefield...just like when I was little.

The kids had to have visitation with their father, so we made a comfortable place for them to stay every other weekend and for one entire month in the summer. He worked at home, so did I. He never visited friends and his divorce tapped him dry financially. He never left the house. There was never a single moment's respite from the constant grind of divorce issues. The ex-wife was livid that Jay's new girlfriend was none other then the dead girl from his past. She knew about me then and was the one who patched him up by marrying him. She would have much preferred him to have a one-night stand with some bimbo. The fact that it was I somehow resurrected in his life and that the kids liked me was particularly chafing to her. She showed her displeasure at every possible turn.

The kids were routinely used as tools to manipulate him to comply with certain outrageous monetary demands. While he was dealing with lawyers and working long hours to try to pay for all of it, I helped as much as I could: with the kids, with money, with paperwork, with birthday parties, with stress management, whatever was needed. It was a bottomless pit that went on forever. His lawyer simply said it was the worst divorce he had seen in his 30-year career. I watched Jay get crucified. It was a nightmare.

The worst torture was when there would be some rug-pulling bomb-shell from his ex, coming out of left field, just before the kids were to show for their weekends. Usually there was not enough time to talk about it or work it out prior to their arrival, so there would be an undercurrent of stomach-knotting stress and unresolved bitterness to suck up. The one thing I would not do under any circumstances was to fight with Jay in front of the children. I didn't care if it killed me. I remembered what it did to me when I saw my parents fight. I wasn't going to do that to these kids; I wasn't going to add to their problems. The emotional toll it took on me to get through those weekends was indescribably hideous. Jay did not know how to fight fair and would pull the angry glare, silent treatment or the under-breath muttering and heavy sighing. I preferred the "up front, get it all out on the table, deal with it and move on" approach to disagreements. That never happened.

To cope with the stress of these bombshells, Jay began drinking heavily, going through suicidal depressions, then the pacing mania would begin. Blasts of anger could not be contained. Boiling, red, hot, anger…directed at me! At times he would forget that it was me and see his ex instead. I had become a prisoner in my own home. There was no place to escape, no place that was safe. The stress was there 24 hours a day, seven days a week. I started to get ill, weird illnesses from the constant, unrelenting, stress; stomach ailments, tooth infections, tendonitis so bad I couldn't lift my coffee cup, had sleeplessness and bad headaches. I felt like I was literally falling apart. Before this I had been the picture of health, I worked out and meditated every day. I felt great.

Aside from all my health problems, something else was beginning to happen. The relentless misery of it triggered the adolescent memories of my parent's own vitriolic and lengthy divorce. So, in addition to the current situation, I had my own subconscious stockpile of divorce memories to deal with.

I remembered being the kid in the middle of the warring parents, I remembered the torture of hearing "your father is a bastard" and "your mother is a bitch." Through the kids' experience I recalled and relived my own experience in every excruciating and painful detail.

Through court delays and attorneys ready for retirement, we were now unbelievably at the bottom of the second year with no end in sight. Jay decided to seek help and get medication for the depression that had now manifested because of the divorce. The doctor gave him Prozac. But it turned out Jay wasn't a depressive; he had bi-polar disorder and Prozac was the very worst thing you could give to someone with his malady.

For the first couple of weeks things seemed better. But then as the medication reached a higher saturation level the Prozac would kick in and work him up to a feverishly "up" level . Later in the day it doubled the effect of his already existing manic condition and he'd be in a state of near frenzy. To bring himself down, Jay would self-medicate with alcohol, something strictly forbidden when on medication of this type. This scenario continued on a daily basis for over six months.

The medication did tone down Jay's anger moderately but he also became a remote emotional zombie. As for me, I watched my peaceful life and quiet home vaporize into this swirl of chaos. I had to do something desperate. I was going down for the count too.

I went to Alanon to learn how to cope with the alcoholism. I got information on detox programs in the area in hopes he would sign up. I thought about doing an intervention on him. But by this time, I was the one that needed serious intervention. I had to get out. But how could I do this? I had my business at the house. I had pets. I had responsibilities and things to maintain. He was simply not capable of taking care of things if I left. How could I leave? I reasoned that I simply had no other choice. My sanity, my health and peace of mind hung in the balance. I had to find a way to get some distance from this insanity.

Because his financial situation was so dire and his credit had been so badly destroyed by his ex, having him move out was not an option; he could not qualify. Besides, I had pity for the children who, after so much time, felt comfortable at my house. I did not feel like displacing them further. I loved them.

The only logical solution was for me to move out of my home! I was now a physical, mental and emotional wreck. I could not manage searching, locating, viewing, qualifying for and moving to a new place myself. I called a friend to help me, my old friend Hank. He was there for me and held my hand through the process.

Miraculously, within the week, I was the hell out of there and into my own quiet and peaceful studio apartment. I drove from my house to work at my home office during the day. I'd also water the lawn, feed the animals, then go home to my apartment at night and recharge for the nest day's onslaught. I stayed there until the divorce was finalized. He was moved out about nine months later and I moved back into my now shabby and neglected home. I did not want to move back. There were too many memories. But I had no choice, my engine was running out of steam.

Moving out was a most serious consequence of my mistake of letting something like this happen in my home. But it also showed me that I could take care of myself if push came to shove.

All in all, that nightmare with Jay lasted nearly three and half years. I tried to weather it the best that I could and see it through to the bitter end, simply because there was no other option. I believe that Jay tried his best, and despite the extreme austerity of the situation, never once shirked any of his responsibilities to his ex or his kids. He always kept his word to them and always did as the court required him to do. We paid a high price, though. It cost us our relationship. I was extremely emotionally and spiritually depleted after it was over. I collapsed and became so physically ill that it took me nearly three years to completely recover. It was a very painful lesson, but a most important one.

Through my experience with Jay, I got to see what I lived with as a child from an adult perspective. I saw once again how angry, divorcing parents could poison every aspect of life. I saw how a father's erratic and angry behavior affected his kids. I HAD BEEN ONE OF THOSE KIDS. Now it all was beginning to make sense.

As a child, I couldn't understand my father's behavior and took it to mean that there was something wrong with me. As I watched Jay go through his ordeal, I started to realize that it was *his* attitude, *his* anger, *his* illness, *his* self-abuse that adversely affected everything and everyone around him. I've heard it said that you can only be as happy as the most unhappy person in your household. I believe that to be true. Misery and depression are diseases that can infect those who come in contact with them. Now I realized what I lived with as a child. It finally all made sense to me.

Chapter 17

He heard me and delivered me from all my fears – Psalms 34:4

WEATHERING THE STORM

*B*ecause years were passing and nobody knew when Jay's divorce would finally be over, it became crystal clear to me that I had to ready myself for the long haul. While I was in exile from my home I had to find something to do to fill the time. Going to the gym had served me well to keep my sanity, but it could only take me so far. I kept having this nagging feeling that life was going on without me and leaving me in the dust. By "accident" I spotted a seminar that promised to help people overcome their fear of public speaking in 3 hours through hypnosis. I signed up. I wanted to conquer this fear once and for all.

It's not impossible to imagine that I would end up suffering from a debilitating terror of public speaking after the kind of childhood I had. All through school I became a master of avoidance by strategically hiding behind the student in front of me, averting my gaze or pretending to be busy. I was already a master at being small and invisible at home. School was relatively easy by comparison. It worked a lot of the time.

As an adult if I ever went to a magic or comedy show where they were asking for volunteers I'd shrink in my chair or look away. If I thought that selecting me was imminent, I'd leave the area entirely and head for the restroom until the coast was clear.

Once, a client of mine asked me to give a small speech about the work I do for a collection of his clients and just the thought of it made me feel nauseous and faint.

I didn't want to feel like this. Many years before, I thought I could force myself to overcome it by by going on a TV Game Show, thinking the lure of money might do the trick. But once they started taping the show, I zoned out and went on "auto pilot." Even though I won a few thousand dollars' worth of prizes, I actually remember very little of the experience.

I once tried "timeline therapy," where, through hypnosis, you visualize your life like a reel of film. Once you've isolated the bad frames, you snip them out and replace them with positive images. It sounded plausible. I really wanted that one to work because it was so expensive.

I could muddle through a business presentation because the focus was not on me, it was on my work. With radio, there was the safety of the recording studio, plus, I could affect a different voice or character. It wasn't really me at all.

There were two incidents that finally prompted me to do something about my fear. The first was an audio-visual presentation, my final exam for the course I was taking. Although I knew the subject matter extremely well, getting up in front of the class proved to be my undoing. My hands shook like I had delirium tremens. No matter how I tried to psyche myself up beforehand, it was to no avail, because now I was automatically going into this anxiety response mode whenever I had to get up in front of people. It wasn't getting better with time, it was getting progressively worse.

The second incident was at my best friend's wedding. Everyone, including the matron-of-honor's 9-year old son, got up to say a few words at the rehearsal dinner...everyone except me. I honestly had a lot to say, as I had known the bride-to-be for many years, but once again, the thought of getting up in front of a group of people was just too frightening. I sat in silence and pretended to have a good time. Not being able to participate in this festive event presented enough incentive for me to find a way out of this life-choking fear.

The evening of the seminar came. I had very high hopes and expectations that I could be cured of my stage fright in this three hour period. I was excited that I could possibly be free that quickly and painlessly. There were at least a hundred people there. I was relieved to see that I wasn't the only one with this problem. But I wondered how all these people were going to be allowed to get up and speak in the short time that we had. Much to my disappointment the teacher turned out to be a pitchman for a hypnosis clinic. Nobody would be getting up to say anything. This "seminar" was in actuality a way to recruit clientele for an expensive series of stage fright "treatments."

While I was there, though, I heard people discussing a well-known speaker's group as a possible way to go. When I got home I made it a point to look into it and found a chapter near me. I decided to bite the bullet and see what it was like while I still had the nerve.

It was worse than I could've ever imagined. The people in this particular group were not just good, they were excellent...every one of them! There were writers, professional speakers, teachers, comedians. I was in awe. I was intimidated. I never wanted to come back. I felt like an old rusty VW trying to get on a speeding freeway of shiny new Jaguars. I was despondent. This was a group of professionals, polished and confident. I was a professional too, a professional tongued-tied, frightened beginner.

Not to be a total coward I did go back a few times. Once, much to my dismay, I was called upon to do a little 2 minute impromptu speech. As I walked up to the lectern, I found that I was actually losing my peripheral vision, my heart was pounding out of my chest, my throat became parched and dry, my body was trembling and my hands and feet were turning cold and numb. In those moments I became acutely aware of how getting up there was affecting me physically and how weird and foreign my own voice sounded to me. I never wanted to feel this way again.

Luckily for me I wouldn't have to. With Jay's divorce issues finally coming to a conclusion, I now needed to use my energies for moving and regrouping my life. Much to my relief, public speaking would have to wait. A part of me was very glad about that.

FACING THE MONSTER

After I moved back to the house, I thought I should get back in action. I didn't want to stay isolated and depressed. I had a lot to do to rebuild my life and I needed all my strength to do that. But Jay, despite his promises to the contrary didn't believe in clean breaks and now saw fit to call me with weekly check-ins which I strongly discouraged. He wasn't getting the message and interacting with him was sapping what little reserves I had left. I put caller I.D. and Privacy Manager on the phone, I'd be screening my calls. I needed to be conserving my energy, not having to babysit him through our breakup.

Although I wasn't feeling up to snuff physically, I talked myself into getting out there and networking. My heart wasn't in it. I really needed a rest but I wanted to get some distance between me and what I had just been through. I had every intention of recovering quickly from my ordeal with Jay and I was going to do everything that I could to accomplish that.

After one of the networking meetings I attended, I received a flier in the mail offering a healing workshop for people who wanted to experience presence, ease and flow when speaking in public. At last! This sounded like something that would honestly help me. I signed up.

The day of the workshop arrived. Just thinking about what I was trying to do put me into a cold sweat even though it was a very hot day. But I had made my mind up that today would be the day. I knew the area and how to get there, but I found myself getting lost. The fearful parts of me were fighting me big time.

There were eight people there. The gentle facilitator explained the rules: We were to softly focus on the speaker; No harsh glares or staring; Only positive feedback once the speaker was finished; As a speaker you had complete freedom to say or not say whatever you wanted. The only requirement was that you had to stay up there your full allotted time and you had to remain there until your feedback and applause were over.

I could feel my heart thumping loudly already just knowing that my time to get up there was drawing nearer. I had a brief thought of leaving and saying I could come back at another time but I stayed put.

Three people went before me. They seemed to manage pretty well and I was happy to see that this was not like the polished professional business speaking group that had intimidated me so much. These were people like me, fellow sufferers of stage fright. Then the moment of reckoning arrived, my name was called. I felt all the things I had come to expect when attempting something like this; the vision impairment, the pounding heart, the parched numbness. I knew my feet were walking but I couldn't feel them. Once I had gotten to the front of the room and saw those faces looking at me, I lost it and started to sob. All I could do was grab the tissue box. It was embarrassing, to say the least. For what seemed like an eternity I couldn't speak. All I could do was cry the whole time, while feeling like someone was punching me in the stomach. I was once again the shamed little girl in the mercado; the humiliated little girl on stage at the recital with everyone looking at me; my dad looking at me. I was quaking and trembling. I felt I would throw up.

Somehow I lasted those first three excruciating minutes, realizing that it was the focus of attention, more than the speaking, that had been my problem all along. After it was over, I found, much to my surprise, that I did not get criticized for a job poorly done. Rather, people said kind things like "courageous" and "honest"; then they applauded. I had to stay in their focus until the applause was finished.

There were two more rounds to go. Difficult, yes, but none as terrifying as that first one. By the last round I actually managed to speak coherently for 5 whole minutes! I got a tremendous amount of loving support and kind feedback. It's what my soul had been craving all along, kindness, encouragement and approval.

By this time, though, I was really becoming uncomfortable because I was beginning to experience the physical manifestations from what had just transpired. My stomach was on fire and my head ached worse than it ever had. By the time it was over I felt like I had been run over by a truck. There wasn't one single part of me that wasn't hurting...on every level of my being. I obviously really needed to do this. What a godsend that this gentle approach was made available to me or I don't know what would've become of me.

When I got home all I could do was crawl into bed. I did not pick up the ringing phone. Jay's problems would have to wait, it was my turn now. I could not eat and I slept for two days. A fractured part of myself was finally beginning to heal. With this one courageous action, I had reclaimed my life and gave myself the greatest gift of all: the chance to live it fully. The shame had been looked at and dealt with and I didn't need to hide anymore.

I had gone as far as I could post-trauma, now I could let myself do what I really needed to do for a long time. I could let myself fall apart.

PART 8: FROM THE ASHES

Chapter 18

Rest in the Lord and wait patiently – Psalms 40:1

PICKING UP THE PIECES

One cannot expect to escape from hell unscathed and I was severely singed. I had been emotionally recovering from my experience with Jay and the aftermath of my tour of duty with him for over a year. I wasn't recuperating as quickly as I had hoped. I was simply worn out from all I had been through and now found it necessary to take a major time-out from life because of my health. It finally broke from so many years of constant stress. I had been pushed too hard and now it was too late. I could no longer force myself to do anything. Add to that the horrors of 9/11 and I found myself pushed over the edge. The reserves I now needed for myself had been foolishly depleted on others. My body was rebelling with heart palpitations, tremors, tinnitus, extreme fatigue, sleeplessness, forgetfulness and inability to concentrate. I had always been capable of taking care of myself but now I couldn't even do that. I didn't have the strength to go grocery shopping or even take out the trash. I was lethargic and slept many hours a day to relieve the symptoms. This went on for months and every doctor I saw seemed to make it worse with every new prescription they wrote. I was extremely weak on every level and much to my horror I found that I couldn't even work. It had become clear to me that the damage done was severe. I had to take matters into my own hands if I was to get well.

To survive financially, I was forced to sell a beautiful and costly heirloom given to me by my aunt. I felt bad to do so, but I literally had no other choice. My life had become much more precious to me and I appreciated her gift all the more for the time it afforded me.

It was discovered that I had chronic fatigue syndrome, adrenal exhaustion and compromised kidney function brought about by stress and the extensive use of the antibiotics and cortisone that had been given to me for such a long period of time for persistent sinusitis. I wouldn't discover until months later, however, that it was the Predisone that proved to be my undoing. Apparently, I had had a severe allergic reaction to it and the balance of my body had been completely upset. I woke up one morning simply unable to move. After much deliberate effort to get to the phone I finally enlisted the help of a kindly neighbor who drove me to Emergency, where I was informed that I had been overdosed. I might've had a good lawsuit. But I was not well enough to even consider it. Lawsuit or not, I had to be able to function. That was my first priority.

To understand what was happening to me, I envisioned it this way; You have a fish tank filled with fish, snails, plants, rocks and water. When it is a completely balanced eco-system, everything thrives. Now imagine pouring a bottle of liquid bleach into that tank. Everything is killed, becoming food for harmful bacteria that consume what should be your nutrients, leaving toxic by-products that your already-weakened body has to process. All you are really left with once you clean it out are the rocks and the tank itself.

Sadly, that was the reality of who I was now: the tank and the rocks. I had the daunting task of completely rebuilding myself from the gravel up. It was going to be a major endeavor. For help, I went to a naturopathic practitioner who outlined a stringent course of treatment for me which I was to follow to the letter.

The foods I could eat were narrowed down to just a few basic things: lean meats, fresh vegetables, unusual ancient grains like quinoa, spelt and amaranth; no fruits, no breads, no vinegar, no sugar, no cheese, no dairy. Plus, I needed to take specialized and costly supplements, for which my health insurance proved useless. I was to have absolutely no stress, do absolutely no physical exercise, as my adrenal glands could not take it. My life had changed drastically.

For months I kept to the prescribed regimen and for months nothing seemed to improve. I didn't know how long it would take to get well and no one seemed able to tell me. I was very frightened that I had irrevocably harmed myself from all the stress that I had allowed in my life. It really was a killer, just like they said it was. All I could do was to continue on this simple path and hope for the best.

During this time I found that I did not care about participating in things of the world. The world had gone mad, things didn't make sense.

My life didn't make sense. I did not care about money, or relationships, accomplishment or past hurts. I simply did not want to play anymore. I was being forced into a major time-out and I had to take it. I had no control over any aspect of this process. I just had to survive the best I could.

When the money from the heirloom sale ran out, my only other option was to take out a second on the house to survive. It was now becoming clear to me that recovery would take longer than I imagined and I worried and wondered if I'd ever get well.

This, I was beginning to realize, was much more than just my response to the Jay divorce and relationship issues. When it came right down to it, I was processing the 50 years of struggle, strife and challenge and overcoming the fears that had been my lot in life. I was just done. A part of me did not know or care if my drive or desire to participate would ever return. I had to leave all that to a higher power and concentrate on my immediate health concerns. My world became very small indeed and would remain this way for quite some time. I had to let go and let God. I would have to learn patience. Slowly, very slowly I began to regain my sense of health and well being.

ASSIMILATING WHAT I LEARNED

Eventually, I came to see the two major relationships since the breakup with my father not as the failures I previously thought them to be. I had learned many things from them. I learned how to really open up and how to survive a breakup; I learned I was capable of commitment; I learned how to be more compassionate. I learned how to distinguish between someone else's emotions and fears and my own. I learned how not to take things so personally. I learned how to give. I learned how to communicate and face conflict. I tried to conduct myself with integrity no matter what the other guy did, knowing that this too would some day end and that I would have to live with the consequences of my conduct. I learned not to speak out of anger. I learned I was capable of protecting myself when and if it became necessary. In short, I learned who I am, what I was made of. These relationships made me strong and, dare I say, fearless in love. I survived the trials by fire. I could survive anything.

CONTINUING EDUCATION

Although I really couldn't accomplish much physically on my own while I was recuperating, it didn't mean I couldn't hire someone else to do the necessary improvements on the house now that I had moved back in. I couldn't stand the place. It was full of unhappy memories. I needed to change things if I was to continue living there. Jay and the kids left it in shambles. The house needed as much repair work as I did.

Hal came over with his partner Craig to give me a bid on the work I wanted done. I really wasn't feeling well that day and actually wanted to cancel.

Hal, although a little rough around the edges, proved to be an articulate craftsman. He had a bright attitude and was full of ideas and enthusiasm. He really knew his stuff and liked what he was doing. I felt he would do a good job as foreman of the project, so I decided to start them out on something small and see how it went.

That small job turned into five months of improvements to the house. Hal and Craig became my trusted and valued friends, day by day. Craig would sometimes bring his wife and kids over and occasionally we'd have a barbeque. Hal would bring his teen-aged daughter to our get-togethers. He proved to be a decent and hardworking man. He had loads of integrity and would actually re-do a job if it wasn't up to his standards. He was always polite to me and I found his humorous antics fun and uplifting. There was no guile or pretense about him. Unlike Jay, Hal displayed a consistency of personality that I had not experienced before and I liked it. I had a great respect for him and I looked forward to seeing him everyday.

Occasionally, as my health began to improve, I'd ask to get involved with the more manageable tasks on my house project and sometimes ended up working with them side by side doing the easier things. At these times I nearly forgot that I was ill. So here at my lowest point Hal and I got to know each other, little by little. I found out that he came from a similar background as I did. But unlike me, he had a tendency to display his anger outwardly and that had gotten him into some serious trouble in the past. If I hadn't known him for so long, maybe that information would've frightened me. But with the foundation we had built, it didn't faze me in the least. I had seen evidence of his temper in action on Craig when he did something inept. But as bad as it could get, it wasn't even close to the fireworks Jay had come up with.

Hal had a lot of pluses; he was not married, he was not in the middle of a divorce, he did not drink, both his children were adults, he had loved his mother, I liked how he looked and I really liked that he could make me laugh. The most endearing thing about him was that he always said "I love you" to his daughter before they ended their conversation. He was a loving individual and someone I wanted to get to know better.

When they were through with my project, I found that I really missed Hal, and he missed me too. Quite often, we'd talk on the phone to catch up on things.

As luck would have it, the neighbors saw the work they did on my house and decided to have Hal and Craig do work for them too. At first it was wonderful to have them so near by. They would invite me over to see what they had accomplished and sometimes I'd invite them over on their lunch break or bring lunch to them.

Unfortunately, the neighbors took issue with the visits and decided to ban everyone except Hal, Craig and their crew from the premises. No one was allowed on their property at anytime, even their families were not allowed. The joyful times had come to an abrupt and cheerless end.

Up until now, Hal had never made any sort of pass at me in all these months, even though I felt he liked me. But now, because we were separated more often, we began to hug each other when we actually got to see one another. Seeing him made my day. We found that we really enjoyed our time working together and even toyed with the idea of possibly going into a sideline business together.

When Craig got wind of this he did not like it one bit. He apparently felt very threatened by my presence in Hal's life and the possibility of losing his meal ticket. Craig began to turn on me and made false accusations that I was out to destroy their business. I was surprised by this, because up until now I had done everything I could to promote them. But he played it to the hilt, and had everyone convinced, including Hal.

I couldn't believe what was happening. These were my friends, I babysat their kids, I invited them into my home, and I worked side by side with them. How could they be turning on me like this? It was unbelievable and unbearable. Craig had Hal thoroughly convinced that I meant to do them harm. There seemed to be nothing I could say or do to prove otherwise. It would be weeks until things would be straightened out and I got to experience first hand the terrifying and destructive power of the spoken word coming from a jealous and angry heart. It was devastating. In time, Hal discovered that he had been played by his partner, and from that moment on their partnership began its downward spiral, two months later our partnership began.

I never so thoroughly loved anyone like I loved Hal. The simplest things were fun as long as we were together. We laughed a lot. Just holding hands with him gave me a feeling of joy and safety. No one ever made me feel like that. As my health began improving, we had the opportunity to work on several small projects together and found that every one we did flowed smoothly and came out beautifully. We had such a strong foundation of trust built slowly over so many months that I couldn't help but feel secure. I came alive around him. I was in heaven and I felt like I had found my counterpart.

Then as unpleasant issues with his partner and their business surfaced and pressed harder upon him, I began to see a change in Hal. He became remote and withdrawn at times. At other times he became agitated and nervous. His partner's behavior upset him so much at times that he'd become nauseous and had trouble sleeping. Then his temper started to flare up…at me and at himself! I was totally taken aback. This couldn't be, not again! He wouldn't talk to me about his feelings, instead he'd withdraw completely and disappear for days. I was heartbroken. This was not the same guy I knew and fell in love with. Where was he?

I went through the torture of these ups and downs, my heart going through yet another excruciating emotional roller coaster ride. Month after month, our relationship spiraling downward in a now predictable pattern; at first the angry flare up, followed by his copious (oh my God, not again!) drinking, self-punishment and isolation, then the recovery and damage control. But the damage control only did so much where our relationship was concerned.

Little by little these actions chipped away at the love and the trust in our once beautiful relationship. Eventually, I had to step back and take a look at things objectively as they really had become. I could come to only one horribly sad conclusion; the Hal I knew and loved was gone, maybe never to return. The imposter in his place was a poor substitute for the magnificent original. I wanted my beloved Hal back. I had no choice but to let this one go.

STILL STANDING

I saw a bit of my former self in Hal. Perhaps that is why I felt so compassionate and patient towards him. I myself needed that kind of patience and acceptance when I was coming out of my long "hibernation." I needed to know that someone loved me no matter what. Hal had not been in a relationship for many years and he had to go through a "cleaning of the pipes," just like I did with Matt, to be emotionally involved with another person.

Hal was never really unkind to me intentionally; that's what made it so difficult for me. He was unkind to himself and that in turn hurt me deeply. By treating himself so badly, he was also treating the one tied to his heart badly too, whether he fully realized it or not. He was not an island, as he sometimes believed himself to be. His actions very much affected others, especially me. But, I could not take that kind of pain indefinitely. I had been through too much and I deserved better. I had already come from a place of self-hatred. I saw the damage and heartache it could produce. By having made the effort to clean up my act, taking the time to learn to love, know and value myself, I was now capable of really being all there for someone else. It was my gift to them.

At the times when he was at peace with himself, nobody loved me better then Hal. It was a very difficult decision to let him go.

LETTING GO

All I ever wanted in my life was to love someone and be loved back. I only wanted my counterpart. But with so many heartbreaks and relationship failures that had become my experience, I had to learn the art of letting go. Sometimes this was difficult because a part of me did not want to let go. I wanted what everybody wants…true love and happily ever after. Sometimes I thought, maybe if I could hang on a little longer, things might change. Of course they never did.

When a relationship had run its course, I would get a feeling of extreme unease and discomfort. It meant the scales had been irrevocably tipped toward the negative side. This was the first indication that something was amiss. I was terrified when this feeling would come because it meant unpleasantness was soon sure to follow, whether I liked it or not. No matter how much I would try to pretend things were normal at this point, it was impossible to go back to the blissfully ignorant state that I had been in previously. It meant that I had outgrown the relationship or it had outgrown me. And unless there were major changes on both sides, that both parties were willing to make, it was on its last legs.

I didn't want to be alone. But when it had been made clear to me that a relationship was not mutually healthy for us anymore, I regrettably had no choice but to let it go.

From a spiritual standpoint you cannot lose what is yours by divine right through the act of release. True release actually opens the way for either what you just let go of, or its equivalent to come your way. This was a hard concept for my personality to grasp. I did not want to let go, ever, but I had to learn it nevertheless. You've heard the lyric, "If you love somebody set them free." I added, "If they come back to you it's meant to be."

SAYING GOODBYE

Over the years I had developed a spiritual exercise to help me process all the losses and heartaches quicker. It was emotionally an extremely difficult exercise, but it was quick and it was thorough. The important part of it was that it couldn't be faked or shortchanged. It had to be done sincerely. I called it "The Train Station." I would sit quietly with my eyes closed and I would play out this scenario:

My partner and I would be sitting facing each other in a gazebo at the Train Station. I would tell him each and every thing that was in my heart to tell him. All the love, disappointment, gratitude, any details that I felt I needed to share would come pouring out with no resistance or interference from the other party. He actually was a passive listener. Sometimes these sessions were so heart-wrenching that I would be sobbing uncontrollably before it was through. After I said what I needed to say, I would walk with my partner to the departing train where he would get on-board. This is the part that could get tough…

In some cases I would hug and kiss him goodbye, or hold on to him for a long time, then I'd watch him go to his seat. Sometimes I would go to the window where he was seated and hold his hand through the open window, running along to keep up while the train started to leave. These were the toughest "deep-in-my-heart" connections to release, the ones that I truly did not want to let go of. Eventually the train would pick up speed and I would have to let go. I would watch it move quickly down the tracks, becoming smaller and smaller until it disappeared behind the mountain. By this time I would be as emotionally spent as if everything I had just experienced had been real. Sometimes all I could do afterwards was to crawl into bed, sometimes for the rest of the day. Only once did something unusual happen…

Let me preface this by saying that no one in twenty years has ever come back into my life on a personal level after I did the train exercise. Usually on a spiritual level everything had been said, done and acknowledged and we both moved on. But in one case, after the train had disappeared behind the mountain, a lone figure came walking back towards me a short time later. It was Hal! I took it to mean that we might still have work to do together. Only time would tell.

BURNT OFFERING

There was another way of releasing, equally as painful and just as thorough. When a relationship was over, there were usually tell-tale signs of it all around the house that may have been collecting for some time. A photo, a pressed rose, letters or cards that at one point meant everything. These were things that had great emotional significance, things that you'd never dream of parting with when the love was strong. I would be compelled to keep some of these articles, as the memories they evoked were pleasant ones. Other reminders may not have been as joyful.

In order to be free of the emotional ties and to aid in letting go, I'd collect one or several of the more important symbols of the relationship. If it was a letter, I might read it a few times, if it was a photo, I'd look at it more closely than I ever had. If it was a mement o, I'd study it and allow myself to remember the details surrounding it. Then I'd build a fire in the fireplace and slowly, deliberately place each article on the pyre. I'd watch it catch aflame, curl, blacken and vaporize into smoke and ash. It was a permanent and irretrievable release.

THE SACRED TRUST

It's taken over 20 years of heartbreak and failed relationships to really know who I am. As a result of that education, I have come to consider a love relationship to be a sacred trust between two people. I believe that for the time we are given together, I owe that person my very best self, consistently. I owe them honesty, fidelity and a compassionate understanding of their problems and fears. I owe them a listening ear and a thoughtful response. I owe them commitment of time and energy even when it gets tough. Each person comes with vulnerabilities and hurts from previous pains and losses. It takes empathy and patience to break through these barriers and come to the safety of now. I consider mutual trust to be of paramount importance and the most precious gift we can give to one another. It is something I will always strive for and it is something I would guard at all costs. If, after giving my very best effort, our mutual spiritual development, peace of mind or emotional security are not attainable or sustainable then I have no choice but to step aside and let go. By giving my very best, I am never really the loser if the relationship fails. I, after all, had the supreme privilege of having been allowed into someone's life, heart and soul. The sharing of genuine love attained through that best effort will always be a part of me and shall forever remain indelibly written on my heart. For that I am truly grateful.

PART 9:
WHERE THERE'S SMOKE

Chapter 19

The meditation of your heart shall give understanding – Psalms 49:3

WHY?

*A*s a child, I remember wanting to know why my parents were so unhappy because I wanted to make it better for them if I could. Over the years, I heard tidbits about their lives, some parts more often than others. But because they were never stories with any real continuity I had to piece it together the best that I could. This is what I know.

WHY DAD?

Dad was the only child of lowly educated, immigrant parents. He was a first generation American. In some bizarre twist of fate, Dad was born with a genius IQ. Frankly, his parents didn't know what to make of him.

It was never a secret that Grandma would've preferred a little girl who she could dote on and dress in frilly things. Many times she said that birthing my father was like giving birth to the devil himself because labor had been so difficult.

She hoped that one day he would become lead window dresser at the May Company. Dad had other aspirations. He found he had an aptitude for science and math. While growing up, there really was no one for him to communicate with on his intellectual level.

Grandma dressed my dad in knickers and sent him to tap school while the other kids played regular team sports. He became the frequent butt of bullying at school. Once he was involved in an altercation at a playground and was the recipient of a swing in the face which twisted one of his front teeth in an unsightly position. His parents never saw fit to have it straightened or fixed in any way.

My grandparents struggled to make it through the Great Depression; my father was eight years old at the time.

Grandma liked silk, satin and lacy underthings, but found that grandpa's income as an auto mechanic was a poor source for such finery. She was a spectacular cook and discovered that others thought so too. She would hire herself out during the holidays preparing elaborate meals for other families while her own husband and son waited in the car until she would finish cooking, serving and cleaning.

My grandfather's only place of solace away from my grandmother was the garage, where he developed a method to make his own mash liquor. He was a kind and simple man with a third grade education. I remember him being soft spoken and loving. He died of cirrhosis of the liver when I was only eight years old.

My father entered the army but did not serve overseas. He instead was stationed in the central west coast where he worked in the medical field conducting experiments on effective insect exterminating substances. He was embarrassed by his unsophisticated upbringing and learned about culture and the finer things in life from a mentor and surrogate father figure.

After his years in the army, my father went to medical school. He was already in his late twenties. As a studious, shy, young intern, he met my mother while she was working as a nurse's aide in the same hospital. She barely spoke English but was Ingrid Bergman-type pretty. He knew he was going places and he felt he could mold her into the kind of showpiece wife befitting a doctor. Love never had anything to do with it.

My father readily admitted that he was not eager to have children, yet despite warnings by his mother-in-law to take precautions against unwanted pregnancy, almost immediately, he found himself with a tuberculosic wife and a child on the way. As an only child, he had no experience with an emotional three-ring circus such as this. His life had become complicated. With the encroaching demands on his time and energies and with no relationship skills he found solace at work and dealt with the emotional complexities of a growing family with anger and impatience. That kept things at a safe distance.

WHY MOM?

I can't tell my mother's story without telling my grandmother's story, because they are so inexorably intertwined. I only know bits and pieces of both.

My grandmother was born of aristocratic German/Russian heritage in 1902. Her family was brutally killed during the Russian revolution when she was 15 years old. Being the only survivor of her immediate family, she was forced to live with her only remaining relative, an uncle, who lived in another town.

Although her upbringing left her bereft of any practical homemaking skills, she was a surprisingly good student and had an interest in becoming a doctor, quite a rarity for women in her time. While in school, she met and fell in love with a fellow aristocrat and they spent their time writing poetry and enjoying each other. (It has been said that my biological grandfather was a famous Russian poet, but it has never been confirmed.) It is rumored they were secretly married. He was sent away to become a soldier. She was left in a family way and my mother was a product of that union. To conceal the perceived illegitimacy, my grandmother married an agronomist (tree doctor) who agreed to take on the added responsibility of my mother.

My grandmother did not let something as small and insignificant as a child get in the way of her medical education. She sent my mother to live with her new husband's family in a nearby village. My mother knew comfort and happiness in the care of her extended family, as they were poor but loving people.

When my mother turned seven, it was decided that she would leave the only family she ever knew and go to live with her mother and stepfather, who she believed to be her real father. Her job was to take care of her new little sister while the parents were out doing their thing. The conditions were not nearly as clean or as loving as her prior living arrangements, and she became deathly ill with dysentery within a short period of time.

She also couldn't understand why her little sister was treated so much better then she was by her father. Her mother knew this and felt guilty about the discrepancy in affection but never revealed the truth.

Grandmother was now making house calls on horseback treating sick people from town to town. Her two girls were left alone a lot to fend for themselves. They were alone at home when the first Russian tanks showed up near to their home in 1942.

A neighbor reported grandmother to the KGB for the stockpiling of goods and food that she had access to because of her station. She was arrested and thrown into jail while her husband was visiting family out of town. Upon his return, grandmother noticed his inappropriate attentions towards my mother who was now 18 year old. Around 1943 grandmother's husband disappeared or was forcibly removed from the house. (There is a theory that he was taken away by the KGB). The girls were forced to leave their home and were shuttled like cattle in railroad cars to an "ordinary displaced person" camp; it was called the "Ouslanders Way Station" for sorting people by ethnic categories. They were given bullet-holed bloody clothes to wear that formerly belonged to the Jews that were incarcerated there. They were given a small flat in which to live. My mother cooked and served the German soldiers while her sister was taught watch repair. Grandmother was performing medical procedures sometimes of questionable morality on the front and elsewhere.

They were moved to different camps many times, including Auschwitz, and somehow they ended up on the trains through Poland, just missing the bombings of Stutgart, Dresden and Prague. Unfortunately, during one of their layovers my grandmother had her left arm blown off by shrapnel and nearly bled to death. All three women witnessed phosphorus bombs where people's eyes were burned white, and experienced much displacement, pain and confusion for five years of the war.

In the fall of 1947, they somehow made it to the coast and boarded a boat to the temporary freedom of Canada. Though nobody knew it yet, my mother was now ill with tuberculosis. In order to be allowed into the country, my aunt pretended to be her sister for the mandatory x-rays; miraculously the trick worked.

After a while all three moved to the northern west coast. My mother, still ill with tuberculosis, got a job at a hospital as a nurse's aide. There she met my father, liked his eyes, brought him a can of peaches as he was studying late one night. She thought this guy was going places. Love never had anything to do with it.

After their marriage, her ill-health created serious problems for everyone. While she was pregnant with me, a pneumothorax needle broke off during a doctor's visit and collapsed her lung. Both our lives were in grave jeopardy. Mother was advised to either abort or stay in bed for the remainder of her pregnancy…she chose the latter. I admire her for choosing that difficult option.

Immediately after I was born, we were separated. I was not placed in her arms; I was not allowed to be next to her. I was isolated and shuttled off to live with my father's mother while my mother recuperated from the TB. Perhaps this lack of early bonding affected our relationship from the very start.

In her-mid thirties, Mother found out that the man she knew to be her father was not in fact her biological dad. Learning this news did something terrible to her psychologically. She desperately wanted to know who her real dad was. No one ever told her.

Despite surface pleasantries, there was a deep-seated contempt between my mother and grandmother, which was hard to hide when they were in close proximity. Their get-togethers would deteriorate rapidly into a mutual bitch session and usually end up with my mother in tears. I never got the impression that they really liked each other, but mother never had the guts to break free from her mother's influence. One of the reasons might have been that my grandmother became a very wealthy woman through real estate, and the promise of inheritance proved to be an overpowering lure to my mother, perhaps overriding a more healthy response to the maltreatment she received.

Grandmother's guilt and overcompensatory behavior to my mother crippled her in many ways. Mother sublimated her true feelings of frustration, anger and helplessness through passive-aggressive behavior. But she found that she could exert the full measure of her wrath and power on weaker personalities like myself. With her own mother she behaved like a trained animal waiting for a treat. It was a dance they agreed to continue until my grandmother's death.

During my grandmother's prolonged illness, my mother tried to take on the responsibility of her care because it put her in position to receive the rewards when the end did come. It was a practical and calculated move, plus it looked good. But the undercurrent of mutual hatred proved to be too much of a strain on both of them.

It was a shock to my mother to find that there was no inheritance. In the end, after all the medical and nursing home expenses were tallied, there was very little left over. And what was left rightfully went to my aunt and her children, who assumed the enormous responsibility of taking care of all of grandmother's needs until her death. The bitterness about this has remained, and the breech between my mother and her sister has become insurmountable because of it.

I wish it could have been different for my mother. I really believe she needed to let go of her mother and find her own way, like I did. But apparently she did not feel she had the strength to do that. The promise of money kept her in bondage.

My mother learned her behavior from her mother. That dysfunction was all she could teach me because she hadn't bothered to learn any other way herself. I fought like hell to break free of it and find another way without guidance or role models of any kind. As I look back, I could've very easily fallen into the same trap as my mother did. It would've been the path of least resistance. But I simply couldn't tolerate the pain and unhappiness and survive in this world.

In a way I felt like I was the unfortunate recipient of all of my family's cumulative, multi-generational dysfunction that had been mindlessly handed down and repeated through the ages. The day of reckoning would eventually have to come and it would have to fall on somebody. It just happened to reach the critical level with me.

It was not an easy position to be born into. It has not been an easy life to live.

PART 10:
THRESHOLD TO HEAVEN

Chapter 20

Look for new heavens and a new earth – 2 Peter 3:18

WHAT I ASKED FOR

I would be lying to you if I said any of this was fun, or that going through all of this was something I wanted to do. As a child I remember wanting to know why. Well, I certainly got what I wanted. I just didn't realize what it would take to get the answers. As I look back on what I know of my parents I could see that the traumas each of them suffered as children had a major impact on their lives, and consequently on their children. Whether they would see it that way is a different matter altogether. I believe a part of them stopped emotionally developing right there and they were stuck just like I was after the incident at the recital and in the mercado. I easily could've remained trapped in that restricted and narrow mode for a lifetime because of fear and parental indoctrination. Without my father's love, acceptance and validation or my mother's consistent, emotional stability, I really didn't stand a chance. Actually, there was really no reason that I should ever have escaped my lot in life. God's grace alone provided me the opportunities to break free from the cycle…if I chose to use them as opportunities to do so. It was always up to me to choose.

It's remarkable to me to discover that every negative experience that I faced; divorcing and going back home to live, the lonely road of reparenting, my cousin's death, my family's reactions, my health crises, and failed relationships were all designed to open my eyes, facilitate my education and subsequent release from the cycle of misery. These were keys to freedom that could've easily been overlooked, faded, and in time, forgotten. If it had been left up to me I probably would've rather chosen to live in blissful ignorance. I would've never wanted to know the truths about my life. Obviously someone else had other plans for me. Maybe this was the plan all along.

ACCEPTING MY LIFE

It took me over twenty years to understand, unravel and overcome the twisted legacy left to me. I had to conquer my heartbreak, my addictions and negative thinking. I had to learn how to take care of myself and learn how to feel again, pain as well as joy. I had to have the courage to free my creativity so as to finally be productive, appreciated and well-paid for my talents. I had to have the courage to open up to give and receive love and compassion, to choose relationships wisely and let them go when warranted. I had to learn how to forgive myself and others completely. I needed to develop my physical, mental, emotional and spiritual selves so they could all work in unison for my benefit. I had to learn, as an adult, what I should've been taught as a child. If I had known the truth of how long this would take when I started the process, I probably would've thought it impossible and not have chosen to press forward. But what a dim future and unhappy life I would've had.

With what I learned over the years, I now believe that both my parents were either afflicted with what I understand to be narcissism and/or manic depression to varying degrees, with a bit of alcoholism thrown in for good measure. Unfortunately for us all, neither ever believed in getting help of any kind. Because of this, I wasted so many years believing that I had no right to be alive. I don't think either of them will ever fully realize how much I gave up to climb out of the pit they created for me. I've tried not to focus too much on what I might've accomplished if I could've fully put my energies into the avenues that I loved. It makes me too sad.

Honor thy parents, as I understood it, proved to be detrimental to me, but overcoming their negative legacy has given me freedom to choose to do things differently.

It might be shocking to hear me say that I am ultimately grateful to my parents for unintentionally setting me on this path by their unloving behavior. Who knows? If I had been given the slightest bit of love, I might've been satisfied with that and never had the courage or felt the necessity to mine the depths of my being for my faith in God and strength of my own character. At this point, perhaps the best way to honor us all is to use these negative lessons for the benefit of others. Then it all would've been worthwhile.

WHAT'S CHANGED

Everything that I placed on my original Wish Board has come to pass.

Some things on that board are just now beginning to manifest in my life. I've come a very long way from wondering how I'll replace the shampoo when it runs out. Through this quest, I have discovered that it is possible to have everything you desire, but you might need to go through some profound personal adjustments to make them happen. You might also need to let certain people, behaviors or things go that are not for your highest good in order to make room for what you really do want. I'm now working on another one for the next 20 years. I now know that with an elevated, heavenly state of mind, all is attainable.

The most amazing thing to me is that for all the changes I've gone through, I've ended up being more myself than ever. Somehow I thought I would be changed; that I'd become someone different. Instead, it turns out that this process has uncovered the real me that had been forced into hiding as a child. The singer, dancer and composer are still alive and well. I use my passion for color and design every day for the benefit of my clients. I love animals and work as a volunteer to help with their care. I still have adventures, though of a more modest variety. I'm energetic and I tend to run, not walk, to my office. I can honestly feel joy and can be silly and really laugh...hard. I feel connected to the Universe and loved by God even when I am alone. I'm happy to be alive!

My quest has allowed me to discover many things about myself that I will take with me on the remainder of my journey: I can truly say I know and I respect myself. I now know without a doubt that I am capable of handling whatever the future has in store for me. These are very important things to know.

I am profoundly grateful that I got off the beaten path and took a far more difficult detour. It led me home.

WHAT ABOUT ME HASN'T CHANGED

At times I get side-tracked by things of interest when I should be focusing on the task at hand. I still work too hard and don't know when to quit. I still want people to be happy and I'm sad when they aren't. I still need plenty of time for thinking and alone time to recharge. It's not beyond me to play hooky from work to go to the book store or the movies to keep my sanity. I still volunteer to do things without thinking it all the way through, sometimes regretting my commitment. I still spend too much on gifts. I'm still not thrilled with incompetence and ignorance. I still disparage bad drivers who cut me off on the freeway. I still have a big problem with cruelty to kids and animals and people who inflict their misery on others.

I'm not a perfect person. I'm only a perfect me with all my imperfections. And what I have to say to that is, so what! So what if I'm not the brightest, the richest, the fastest, the prettiest, the bravest, the most educated, the most accomplished kid on the block. So what! Where is it written that one has to be all those things to be worth something? Who says I have to be all these things to be loved? I am who I am and that's more than alright with me...FINALLY!

THE BOTTOM LINE

I've heard it said that our parents are masters of what we are to overcome. If that is true, then I feel I have overcome my masters. I am not angry at my parents. On the contrary. As a child I loved them and was always aware of their unhappiness. I remember wishing I had the power to make it better for them and I would've gladly taken their hurt upon myself rather than see them suffer. In a way, for a while I did just that by trying to live life their way. It didn't work. When it became clear to me that they themselves did not know any better, it became necessary for me to separate from them to protect myself from harm, intentional or not, as I went through these fragile relearning experiences. In the process, I found that my mental and emotional health had become more important to me than their love or approval. The bottom line was that their actions, or lack thereof, forced me to look elsewhere for love, comfort and spiritual understanding. It was a surprise to me to find all these things by looking deep within myself.

At this point I feel a healthy neutrality and detachment about my parents. Neither love nor hate. I am grateful for this hard-won state of mind. It feels okay and I can live with it. Although I will never forget, I harbor no bitterness or resentment towards them. I choose to take the best of each of them with me into the future and leave the rest behind. They gave me what they had to give and I made the best out of the negative lessons they taught me. But now I'm done with it. I never want to look back. It's finally my turn, because I'm now 53 and fresh out of hell.

IN CLOSING

I now believe that I could've gone through the "reparenting" process much quicker had I known that the ultimate goal was a solid foundation of self-acceptance and resulting peace of mind. All I really had as my guide was the intense desire for the freedom from crippling mental and emotional pain. I actually had no idea that I was trying to accomplish this while I was going through it.

If there had been a book such as this, I probably would've worn it out because I needed to know that I wasn't the only one going through hell; not the only one who grew up in this acerbic mulch. That's why I decided to write this book. Perhaps my insights and experiences will help someone else climb out of their darkness and into the light.

It doesn't matter who or what's making you miserable, you can overcome it and have the full, happy life and peace of mind you dream about. It doesn't have to remain a dream. If you can think it, you can make it real. You are in control of your life whether you know it yet or not. DO NOT GIVE UP! NEVER GIVE UP. Use the negative experiences in your life and learn what they are trying to teach you. In reality they are your stepping stones to a more rewarding and enlightened life. Don't avoid your fears, instead, use them as your guide out of unhappiness. Treat yourself with as much love and kindness as you can muster, so that you can release that magnificent child that resides within you still.

I believe I learned, lived, processed and overcame my fears and challenges just to show others like myself that there is a way out of hell.

Remember,
God loves you,
God is guiding you,
God is showing you the way

WE START AGAIN...

THE FINAL CHAPTER

Final Chapter

Whoever loses his life will preserve it – Luke 17:33

A TIME OF TESTING

*S*hortly after I finished this manuscript. I found out that my aunt had been forced into the hospital because of a long standing heart condition. Though it wasn't immediately life threatening, the condition wasn't improving. Of course I was very concerned, but more than that, as we spoke I sensed enormous sadness and guilt in her tone and as I pressed her about it, I found that it had to do with my mother.

The sisters had not spoken for 16 years. The deep gash from the wound at my cousin's funeral never really healed. In its place only distant memories of the sister she grew up with and the lingering bitterness of willful stubbornness and betrayal on the day she was needed the most. She mentioned a birthday card she received from my mother earlier that year that had an unusual tone of apology and deference, also hinting at illness. Was this a plea for forgiveness? Was this her attempt to finally reach out, using sympathetic undertones to soften the approach? I asked my aunt if she had responded and she replied that she was not strong enough to do so emotionally or physically.

After our conversation I deliberated a long time on what to with this news. I was dismayed at what seemed to be my only logical solution. *I would have to facilitate a meeting between the two sisters!* I would be the only one that could do it. Neither of them would ever follow through or make the effort required. It was not inconceivable that this impasse could continue indefinitely and one or the other could die without hope of reconciliation. Then there would be only regrets. With illness on both sides and each afraid or too prideful or hurt to approach the other, it would be up to me to have the strength to bring a resolution of some kind to this lengthy stand-off.

This, of course, was a frightening prospect for me on many levels. What about me? Would I be emotionally strong enough to handle something with this much potential for disaster? Except for superficial exchanges, I had not really spoken to my mother for 16 years either. What about the physical aspects of the trip; The expense? The distance? The bad weather, my poor night vision in areas unfamiliar to me? Not to mention my reduced stamina from the Prednisone. How would I deal with my aunt and her medical issues and sensitivities? What if there was an emergency? What if the shock proved to be too much for them and someone died? How would I react to seeing my mother again after all this time? All these things swirled in my mind like a bad B-Movie.

The thing that had me most concerned about this whole plan, however, was my mother's legendary ability to cancel on a whim at the last minute. With this much time, energy and expense, this kind of behavior would be unacceptable and beyond my capacity to endure. So in remembering lessons from the past, I opted to handle the potential for her disappearing act by omitting the fact the my aunt would be accompanying me, thus lessening the possibility of her cancelation.

I called my mother and told her I would be coming up to visit her at the end of the month, thus giving her plenty of time to prepare. She was not curious why I would be coming up and I did not volunteer. It was a brief call without a lot of chit-chat but she sounded upbeat about it nevertheless.

As the time of the trip was drawing near, I began to have sleepless nights and started to feel sick and nervous. I questioned the sanity of going through with it many times. I had been comfortable away from my mother. I had accomplished a lot and finally felt good about myself and my life. I no longer wanted or needed her approval or her love. In fact, I wanted nothing from her. Then, I reasoned, maybe this was the best place to be emotionally for a mission like this.

The day for the journey finally arrived. In order to mentally process it and not get overwhelmed I had to put it as a list of things to to:

    1) Pack For Trip,
    2) Get to Airport,
    3) Check in Baggage,
    4) Get On Plane,

5) Fly On Plane,
6) Go to Baggage Claim,
7) Get Bag,
8) Pick up Rental Car,
9) Drive to Aunt's House,
10) Stay Overnight,
11) Leave with Aunt in AM,
12) Drive 200 miles to Mother,
13) Visit with Mother,
14) Stay in Local Hotel Overnight,
15) Drive Back to Aunt's House,
16) Stay Overnight,
17) Drive Back to Airport,
18) Get Luggage,
19) Get Ride Home,
20) Get Home,
21) Kiss The Ground,
22) Collapse and Cry if Necessary.

Just 22 little steps to do...Piece of cake! Number 13 was a little dicey, but it's only one step of the 22.

Other than the wet weather, the poor maps, the road construction and inadequate parking, steps 1 through 9 were almost pleasant. When I did arrive, I was immediately struck by the musty, memory-provoking smell of my aunt's moldy, old apartment building and the fact that I had to sleep in my deceased cousin's room. Neither of these things did anything to alleviate the trepidation that began to grow in my heart. Although my aunt and I were very happy to see each other there was a palpable under-current of anxiety for what we were going to attempt the next day. We were both nervous as we didn't know what to expect or anticipate. Actually we were more like prisoners preparing to go in front of a firing squad. I prayed a lot and did my best to sleep that night.

In the morning I had the indescribable need to be comforted. My aunt had the warmth and generosity of spirit to hold me like her own tender child. In that moment she was the mother I never had. I hadn't had many moments like this in my life, where I could simply relax, be held and let myself be loved by someone I trusted. It felt like heaven. We both found ourselves crying over the pain we each had endured for so long. She, over the loss of her daughter and her sister, and I, over the loss of my cousin and my mother. Then we courageously prepared for our journey. It was just a matter of hours now.

The closer we got to our destination the more nervous we both became. I suggested we stop for a light lunch. I could give mother a call and tell her it would be soon now. Her voice sounded happy and strong. Now I started to feel bad about the deception of not telling her about having her sister with me. But I was committed. I would have to follow through with it, so I held my tongue. Too late to turn back or change strategies now. I reminded myself that there was a reason I had to do it this way.

After a lunch that barely stayed down, we proceeded with the remainder of the drive. My aunt and I anxiously clutched hands, virtually white-knuckling it all the rest of the way. We discovered that the roads in this rural area were poorly marked, which made the house hard to find and the addresses hard to read, we had to double back a couple of times. Then through the trees, I saw a grey, ghostly figure in a full-length pink housecoat. But this couldn't be my mother! This person looked older than my grandmother after her long period of illness. Where did that strong voice on the phone come from? I parked the car behind the trees to conceal my aunt and I bravely approached my mother alone. I hugged her politely and she invited me in.

At this point I knew it was my job to tell her that the sister she hadn't spoken to in 16 years was in the car. I broached the subject tentatively, saying that the real reason for my visit was my concern about her relationship with her sister and I wanted to do something about it before it was too late.

Just by mentioning her sister's name my mother's eyes grew wide and in a childishly defensive stance she blurted, "I don't know what her problem is with me, I've tried with her. I don't know what her problem is." It was like watching an eight year old in a playground tussle. Realizing she wasn't getting it, I said "No, you don't understand, she is here. She's been ill, her heart's not strong and didn't feel that she could drive here alone. I picked her up and she is here in the car." Now, I was waiting for the reaction. Would it be a hurricane, a heart attack or happiness, I simply couldn't know. I held my breath. Eventually the full impact of what I was saying hit her. In that moment her eyes became wide with comprehension and she nearly bulldozed me to get to her sister. "She's here, she's here, oh my God, where is she?" Of all the reactions I could've hoped for this one was definitely at the top of my list.

I ran out to pull the car up into the driveway, calming my aunt, who now was in a full state of terror and apprehension as I was doing so. As I pulled to a stop, I just had to get out of the way as they embraced and talked and laughed as they went inside, ignoring me completely. I knew this could be one possible scenario so I contented myself with photographing some of the animals that were roaming about and reading the newspaper in the car while trying not to take the indifference too personally. Could I really expect anything more?

Their reunion went on for over an hour. Then I was invited in. Both were smiling now, although Auntie looked a bit strained. My mother and I talked about the one safe thing that we could discuss...art. She showed me her latest, beautiful work and presented me with a hastily-wrapped gift. A coffee table book on the Art Deco period. As I thanked her, without a word, she pointed to the discarded wrapping paper and ribbon on the table. I thought she meant for me to throw it out, so I gathered it up. "No," she said, "There's something else in it." I looked through the wrapper and saw nothing. Then she pointed strongly to a clump of scotch tape just below the ribbon. Upon further investigation I found it to be a rather large, pale blue gemstone. I was astonished to find such a costly and rare jewel to be so unceremoniously presented. It could've been so easily tossed away in the trash without a second glance...just like me. But how ironic that my journey began searching for the jewel within and now it ended with this gem from my mother of all people. This was indeed full circle I thought . As I sat in a circle with my aunt and my mother in what was once the dining room, I couldn't help but notice the dusty, cob-webbed, piles of books, boxes and brown shopping bags filled with empty wine bottles and beer cans stowed in a corner of the kitchen. There was a look of benign disregard everywhere. As I sat there and politely listened to their banter and tolerated their inside jokes, I was struck by the magnitude of the fact that THIS COULD'VE BEEN ME had I stayed on the path that I had been set upon. In that moment I was so grateful for my life and the struggles and the courage to do it differently.

My mother's beauty had now faded, her health compromised after years of neglect and self-abuse through alcohol and negative thinking. She commented on how young I looked and joked "Botox." It never occurred to her that it was because I chose to take care of myself; that the body reflects the mind.

Near the end of our visit, mother asked, "Who's idea was this?" I gulped hard as my aunt responded, "Your daughter's." "Here it comes," I thought. But to my astonishment, as mother looked me in the eye for the first time on this visit, she matter-of-factly said, "Well, now you've done your good deed for a lifetime." Shortly after that we said our good-byes...Perhaps, I thought, for this lifetime. I felt a sadness and disappointment rather than surprise at the lack of warmth and attention. Despite the month-long lead time, there were no preparations for my first visit in 16 years. I thought how, if the situations were reversed, I would've done it differently...a welcome fit for a queen.

When it was over, my aunt and I breathed a sigh of relief but were both disturbed by what we saw. I had thoughts of bulldozing Mother's place and making it nice for her, get rid of the barnyard animals and the clutter. But I know that would not be appreciated and in fact very much resented. My mother was living how she chose to live. It was the fantasy from her childhood when she remembered being happiest on the farm with her grandma. Who was I to judge her choice? All we could do was to accept it and go on to our lives.

Despite a frightening torrential downpour on the way back to the airport. Steps 14 through 21 were a piece of cake in comparison to the visit with Mother. And I found that once I got home I did not have to collapse and cry. On the contrary, in retrospect I found that I was glad to have made the effort to facilitate the restoration of their relationship even though there was very little in it for me. There was a sense of completion and accomplishment in reuniting these two who could understand one another like no one else on this earth.

On the flight home, though, it occurred to me that perhaps I had been a disappointment to my family in general. For once I had acquired the nerve to break away and begin working on myself, I had changed my position and assigned role of sounding board and negativity receptacle. Because I dared to want something more than that, I changed the familial hierarchy, causing a kind of ripple effect throughout our enjoined emotional fabric. But in doing so, I had eliminated my own job within the family unit. I was no longer appealing and had outlived my usefulness.

Others more suited to the role had now taken my place. Because I had emotionally left the fold, such as it was, I had become an outcast...the proverbial black sheep. So this is what it felt like to want to get healthy and go against the grain!

Afterwards, perhaps foolishly, in trying to keep a lighthearted line of communication open, I sent Mother a rather large and costly pastel set. It took days to research and locate just the right one. I wanted to support the one safe and neutral thing we shared and were comfortable with. Mother did acknowledge receiving the pastels, but explained that she already had several and wanted me to return them for a refund. I arranged to have them shipped back and because I could not return them decided to give them to a very talented artist I know, who was very appreciative. In the meantime I have come to terms with the severe limitations of this relationship...

> *There is a woman I know who went through hell to birth me.*
> *Who was beautiful and talented*
> *Who had the world in her pocket*
> *Who could light up a room with her presence*
> *But who chose instead to live in the dark*
> *How I have missed her all my life...*
> *This stranger... who was my mother.*

MINING FOR THE GOOD

A friend of a colleague was offering an artists' empowerment group to help people realize their creative dreams. When I told her about my writings she simply asked, "Have you written your parents a thank you note yet? Frankly, I must confess that it hadn't crossed my mind to do so...A thank you note? For what?

The more I thought about it, the more I realized how difficult it would be, so it probably meant that I would have to do it. To get through all the challenges and get to a peaceful place despite them was one thing, but to thank them? That was going to be something else altogether. I sat at the computer for a long time trying to come up with something honestly positive to say that didn't sound contrived or inappropriate. For a long time, there was nothing but a feeling of revulsion for challenging myself to do this and the fact that maybe I hadn't come as far as I thought I had. But after much deliberation, this is what came to the page:

Father,

To put it plainly—our relationship has never been an easy one. As a child I desperately wanted what every daughter wants from her father, emotional validation and loving warmth to give her wings.

I spent decades struggling with and grieving about what I never received from you and it colored everything in my life …especially in my relationships with men.

I've done a lot of growing and changing over the years and I have come to terms with many things. Thankfully one of them was learning how to forgive my ignorant mis-steps along the way.

At this point, I can see why it all has been necessary towards the goal of my ultimate development. With sincerity, I can say "Thank You" to you, my father. Although I may have wanted you to be different with me, it is by being precisely who you are that started me on the path urging me to mine deeply for spiritual and emotional reserves that I never would've known I had. This led me to the greatest discovery of all—self-knowledge and acceptance.

Now I can appreciate the good things that we share, curiosity about life and a love of learning, an appreciation of the written and spoken word, a diligent work ethic, a regard for exquisite design and a sense of adventure. I am grateful for these things and I take them with me into my future.

I wanted you to know and I wish you well.

Your daughter

This letter was so difficult for me to write that I had to lie down for the remainder of the day. It took everything I had to reach that deep to find something good to say. In the two remaining weeks until Father's Day, I polished and edited and polished some more. I mailed the letter to Dad for Father's Day. To this day I have heard nothing back nor do I expect I will.

It did occur to me, given our past history with letters, that he might choose to reject it, correct it, leave it unopened, send it back or trash it. I couldn't begin to guess. As of this writing, it has been 8 years since our last correspondence. Perhaps the things I had done in the past had been so unforgivable that I deserved to be written off by him. It was easy for me to imagine him dismissing it with a disdainful comment like, "Oh, you poor thing," and have it be okay. Nevertheless, I wanted him to know that there was some good before it would be too late, whether he could ever acknowledge it or not.

However, I accomplished something else with its sending. I got the strong sense that the spell was finally broken. No longer would I need to repair my relationship with him through surrogates. In fact, I believe that the ones I found so compelling in the past would no longer even be attractive to me. There was nothing more to "fix." With my release of the bad and acknowledgement of the good, I had created a paradigm shift in my life.

A SPECTER FROM THE PAST

Around my birthday I was delighted to receive happy e-mail wishes from my younger brother. We were finally opening up a healthy line of communication and it felt good. As it was a lengthy note, I decided to scroll down to the end to see if I had time to read it or if I needed to get back to it when I returned from a pending meeting.

At its end, I couldn't believe what I saw! An attached letter to him from my father, so vicious, mean-spirited and blame-ridden in its tone that it stopped me dead in my tracks and vortexed me back 32 years to my 21st birthday! Back then, I had been the recipient of that same kind of unforgiving, merciless, cataloging of faults. My mind was aswirl with unpleasant memories and stomach-churning nausea. NOTHING HAD CHANGED AT ALL IN 32 YEARS!! My whole body was trembling as I dialed a trusted friend. I simply couldn't deal with this sudden emotional trauma alone. I read the letter to my friend who was a father himself. After its conclusion, I asked if he would ever write such a thing to his children. "Absolutely not!" was his reply. I wrote my brother back and tried to encourage him not to take Dad's contentious faultfinding to heart. I don't know if it helped. It took me several days to calm myself down.

BACK TO THE MINE

Mother's birthday was coming up and I needed to finish my "assign-ment" of writing her "thank you" letter. I found that I had to come from a somewhat different perspective and although there were similarities in areas, this one proved to be equally as difficult to write as the one to my father.

Dear Mom,

I feel that I have come to the end of a five decade-long struggle into wholeness. Since your's and Dad's divorce, I've been trying to make sense of a life which seemed to be one full of bitterness and anger. When I realized that you and Dad had your own issues to deal with and couldn't really help me, I had no choice but to emotionally go out on my own and somehow make my way in this world, essentially alone. It's been frightening, lonely, and challenging to say the least. I felt much hurt, did much grieving and made many mistakes along the way.

But I've also done a lot of growing and changing over the years and I have come to terms with many things. I've come to accept my life and I've learned how to forgive my ignorant mis-steps along the way.

At this point, I can see why all the pain has been necessary towards the goal of my ultimate development. I've learned that "Life" is the important part. What one does with that life is up to the choices they make. Hopefully I'm making better choices now.

You had a difficult choice to make 53 years ago, one that was frightening and painful I'm sure, considering your health issues at the time. And despite others' warnings to the contrary you chose to proceed. For this I am grateful and I wanted to say "Thank You" to you, my mother, for the courage to go through with a difficult pregnancy to give me life.

We've had our difficulties since then. I may have wanted you to be different with me as I was growing up and becoming an emerging adult, but it's by being precisely who you are that started me on the path, urging me to mine deeply for a spiritual reserve that I never would've known I had. This discovery led to the greatest gift of all—self-knowledge and acceptance.

Now I can appreciate the other gifts we share, a love of music, color and animals, creative problem solving and humor. I take these things with me into my future, wherever that may lead.

I wanted you to know that I appreciate and thank you for that tough choice you had to make so many years ago.

Your daughter

I sent this letter to her on her birthday. Several weeks later, I received a 9 page double-sided, "dissertation" scrawled in pencil on a telephone notepad telling me that I was "wrong," that it was my presence within *her* that kept *her* alive. Then it detailed and recounted *her* experiences of my birth and the unkind actions of those around *her* and that *she* had 500 pages more. There was nothing new here. Though the note was at times very emotional, there was not one single mention of any thing to do with me or acknowledgement to what I had so painstakingly written. I wanted to feel touched, but frankly, it left me flat. I reread it several times, thinking maybe I missed something. Had I really been that unclear in my communication? Was I being selfish in wanting these things addressed? I wanted to scream, BUT WHAT ABOUT ME?!! WHAT ABOUT MY FIVE-DECADE-LONG STRUGGLE?! DIDN'T YOU SEE ANY OF THAT? I don't know what I ultimately hoped to accomplish with these letters. Perhaps it was my last attempt at getting through to my parents before being finally able to let them go. I had to realize that despite my very best efforts, I could not get through to them and I felt very foolish at my dogged persistence in trying to make two venemous cobras into a pair of cuddly bunny rabbits. OK, I GOT IT! Message received loud and clear. For the briefest moment I contemplated writing back to my mother. I let the moment pass as I found that I really had nothing to say. It was time to move on...let's get on with it.

SOME UNFINISHED BUSINESS

The day before Thanksgiving, I returned from a joyful lunch with my remarkable editor to find a message on my answering machine from none other than my mother! This was very unusual, as it was not a tradition by any stretch of the imagination. She sounded quite upbeat about a trip she would be taking to my brother's house in a couple of days and wished me a good holiday. Although the message did produce a reflexive anxiety knot in my stomach, I dismissed it. This sounded safe and neutral enough, so I centered myself, took a deep breath and returned the call to wish her a good trip and a happy holiday as well. Within minutes, our neutral small talk degenerated into what I can only describe as a covertly hostile, passive-aggressive "fishing expedition" with undercurrents of suspicions about my aunt, insinuations about me and dismissive remarks about my younger brother, all thinly veiled with sarcastic questions and nervous laughter. How come I had never been able to hear so clearly between the lines before? After the call, I had to collect myself and regain my balance for the remainder of the day. What the hell was that? I felt like I had been pummeled by a verbal Kung Fu master. I was no match for this. Then I recalled my aunt's brave efforts to make peace with this woman and my brother's idealistic love for his mother and now I was somehow to blame...for what? For opening up the line of communications and sharing, like families do? I couldn't even begin to guess, but here it was again. The guesswork, the mind-reading, the inferred blame. Whatever brief joy I had experienced that moming had evaporated within minutes of my conversation with her. How could I pretend to have a Happy Thanksgiving now? What was it about this particular holiday anyway?

I called my aunt for relief. She would understand. I needed someone to help me through this now all-too-familiar pain. In retrospect, I believe it was a good thing that there had been no answer. I really didn't want to relive that conversation and risk making yet another person unhappy. I felt myself sinking into despair. After all I had been through? I didn't want to feel like this. Please make it stop! For a time, I went on auto-pilot and reverted to my past childhood training; a small part of me wanting to call my mother back; wanting to say to her *"Mama, I'm sorry...for everything. I just want to be able to talk to you again. I'll agree with you. I want to be able to trust you. I want to make it right between us. Please let's make it right. I want it back the way it was when I trusted you; when I loved you, before I had to protect myself from you."* In essence, I had become the little girl again, needing my mama to be the one I ran to, not the one I was running from. These thoughts pressed harder and consumed my mind as the afternoon wore on. I was powerless against this force. All I could do was just to allow myself to feel the pain, the loss, the disappointment and the emptiness. I had no choice but to feel these things and to pray that the feelings would pass. Thank merciful God they did pass. But ultimately, the end requisite was still the same. I could not go back. And now I had just discovered that I couldn't even pretend to tolerate it anymore.

I then remembered something I once read. **You can *choose* to be the victor. You do not have to remain the victim of circumstances.** I began to search my soul for my pathway to peace out of this sudden mental and emotional upset and confusion. Then I found myself calmly sitting down and writing a note to my mother telling her what *I* wanted. I had never explicitly done that before. Now it was time. It read:

Mom,

    After our last conversation, it has become clear to me that I need to respectfully ask that you refrain from communicating with me from now on. This has become necessary for my physical and emotional health. Forgive me—it is not my intention to be unkind, but my well-being is now of paramount importance to me and I am asking for your cooperation. Thank you and I do wish you a pleasant trip.

    Your Daughter

On the day after Thanksgiving, (which incidentally turned out to be one of the most pleasant ever, thanks to my wonderful friends and the genuine emotional work I had done) I sent the note Priority Overnight, to ensure its arrival before her departure. I couldn't risk losing my nerve.

Now I had one final thing to do. To help myself complete the letting-go process, I found it emotionally and psychologically necessary to do something externally to mark the end of the past and to signify a new beginning. I felt it was necessary to inform family members of the changes so that things would be made clear to them and future interactions would be less stressful and awkward for us all. I wanted no misunderstandings or unpleasant communications from uninformed and unaware family members. This is an edited version of the Declaration I sent to each of them:

My Declaration of Independence

*Let it be known that as of this day, I, **Alyson Kay**, officially divorce myself from both biological parents.*

The irreconcilable differences between us have been in the making for 53 years and I now declare that it is over.

The new rules are:
1) No discussion about either of
these individuals to me at any time.

2) Any family member, other than the aforementioned,
wishing to offer encouragement and positive communications,
may do so via regular mail until further notice.
Any others will be returned to sender.

3) If you do not agree with this action, respectfully keep it to yourself.

4) If you choose not to communicate with me or are uncomfortable with these new rules I will understand and I wish you well.

*I love you and I thank you in advance
for your compassionate understanding.*

This had become my new reality. For once in my life I had the courage to plainly state what I wanted and needed. It simply was not up for discussion, opinion or review. There was no one to confer with about this. I would have to muster the courage to do this myself. I deliberated for most of the day as to whether to send it or trash it. I asked the universe for unmistakable guidance. Then, as I was trying to relax with the newspaper, something in my horoscope (of all places), caught my eye and pushed me over the edge of my fear. It was a story illustrating persistence under duress as told by Christopher Walken's character in the movie *Catch Me If You Can*. "Two little mice fell in a bucket of cream, the first mouse gave up and drowned, the second mouse wouldn't quit. He struggled so hard that eventually he churned the cream into butter and crawled out." The astrologer then offered his suggestion, "I urge you to make that second mouse your role model in the coming days."

Immediately I was energized into action; now clear about what I had to do. It was time to wrest away control over *my* joy and *my* sanity, from those whom I now finally recognized as two immature, recalcitrant eight year old bullies, masquerading as parents.

I prepared each copy, wrote brief notes of explanation, and proceeded to mail the Declarations.

After its writing, I realized the enormity of what I had done, and the symbolic importance of this Declaration. Before, although I had, for all intents and purposes, emotionally divorced my parents, no one else knew. They just thought I was being antisocial or unforgiving. This left me open for unwanted and painful communications and allowed me to be drawn back into the fray. Of course, I understood that there was a very good chance that I could lose what was left of my family...again. After all, they could very well be thinking, "Oh no, here she goes again, making trouble. Why can't she just let it rest?" My answer would have to be, "BECAUSE MY LIFE HANGS IN THE BALANCE, THAT'S

WHY! BECAUSE RIGHT NOW I CANNOT BE SORRY FOR THE INCONVENIENCE TO YOUR SENSIBILITIES. BECAUSE I AM FIGHTING FOR MY LIFE HERE!"

Only time will tell if I have any supporters. But in truth it doesn't really matter.

As expected, completing this last painful step with my parents triggered many old feelings to resurface; feelings of grief and sadness for a childhood lost and about parental love that would never materialize. Why couldn't it be safe to be myself, be loved and have a family too? It was sobering to see how things actually turned out without the assistance of hope or selective amnesia or rose-colored glasses. I do not expect the pain of disappointment and loss to ever go away completely. But understanding myself as I do, I know that I will eventually learn to live with it and one day it may even become manageable. The only thing that gives me any comfort at all is knowing that I did the very best that I could without a road map of any kind. This multi-decade process was more than difficult. Coming through this hell intact was an undeniable miracle.

Through these experiences I've learned that I can no longer worry about what others do or don't do, or care what they think about me. I've had to reach so deeply beyond my own endurance and perceived limitations and comfort level that I scarcely recognize myself. I have to wonder what God is preparing me for. Until that answer becomes clear, I will have to content myself in knowing that I have done my best and I can go on from here...

...It may take some time, but...

...I will start again

Epilogue

I now believe that clinging to the minute shreds of false hope over the years proved to be my greatest undoing. That, and my inability to acknowledge the true nature of the actions leveled at me because of who those actions came from.

But cutting the parental "discord" with my final Declaration would not have been possible without the enormous emotional work I had done over the years. When that final moment to act came, I could've easily crumbled, acquiesced and let it slide until the next onslaught. But something happened to me during the course of this journey out of hell; my life and peace of mind became important to me and I finally had enough courage and strength to claim it! Who would've thought the timid, little mouse would learn to roar.

If there's one message I can impart, it's this: Nothing good or beneficial can come from telling a child that they were a mistake, unwanted or a burden. Even if it were remotely true, I need to say as strongly as I am able to on this printed page, **"KEEP IT TO YOURSELF!"**

If there are marital, emotional, mental, financial, or any other adult problems or challenges, "DO NOT BURDEN YOUR CHILDREN WITH THEM!!" I beg you to get appropriate, qualified help to deal with it, whatever *it* is. There is no shame in needing help, we all do at times.

It is an ultimate act of cruelty to make a child to feel as if they have no right to be alive, or to lead them to believe that they were born only to serve their parents' needs and egos. It is an insidious life-leaching legacy that goes contrary to the very nature of the expansive universe itself. It is beyond cruel.

To me, parenting is the most important job there is and shouldn't be taken lightly. Parents are not just birthing flesh, they are creating the hope of our future as human beings on this planet. It is an awesome responsibility. I hope that through reading *Fresh Out Of Hell*, mothers and fathers might be made aware of how unconscious parenting and the way they handle certain key events in their child's life could negatively impact their children's future in ways they never could imagine.

To quote my father, "None of you suffered from any reasonable want." While it's true we had food to eat and a roof over out heads, I beg to differ with his idea of want. Children need love and warmth and positive attention to thrive. It is not unreasonable to crave love, we are wired that way. Without it, children are like flowers in the desert. If they're lucky they might find a tiny footing in the fissure of a rock, out from which they might subsist, but they might never bloom in such a harsh and unforgiving environment. It makes me wonder how many great thinkers, writers, humorists, artists, inventors and other magnificent beings are trapped and buried under the emotional debris from toxic parental influences. What a waste of these precious resources.

We all know there are many forms of child maltreatment. Sexual abuse is a most heinous breach of trust and an unspeakable violation. Physical abuse closely follows suit. According to ASCA (Adult Survivors of Child Abuse) the many participants who suffer from these forms of abuse have found that their *emotional* abuse issues have been the most difficult to work through and recover from. Just because the scars from emotional abuse are externally invisible does not make its repercussions less debilitating, perhaps even more so.

For the adult survivors of childhood emotional abuse, please take heart. When I first started this process of healing, I thought I was on my own in dealing with my problems. I did not know that resources and help were available. At that time there was no such thing as the Internet. Today it's a very different story. There are many avenues out of dysfunction, the book stores are full of thousands of wonderful self-help and inspirational books written by caring psychologists, ministers and Ph.D's. Pick one and really follow it through. Get the help you need. Find the group or the counselor or the organization that is a fit for you. When you've gotten what you've needed from that one, go to the next...YOUR PATH IS THERE IF YOU LOOK FOR IT! Make the commitment to the most important person in the world...you. Do not stop until you have arrived at your destination of self-acceptance and wholeness. Accept nothing less.

Resources

ADULT SURVIVOR SUPPORT

The Morris Center – *www.ascasupport.org*
A nonprofit organization providing a support program Adult Survivors of Child Abuse, ASCA, sexual and/or emotional child abuse or neglect. Its web site contains materials that can be downloaded, a monthly newsletter, and an ASCA e-meeting all for free.

www.controllingparents.com
A site dedicated to providing support and resources for adults raised with unhealthy control.

National Clearinghouse on Child Abuse and Neglect –
www.nccanch.acf.hhs.gov
The Clearinghouse offers a bibliographic database of child maltreatment and related child welfare materials, summaries of State laws concerned with child abuse and neglect and child welfare, fact sheets, resource lists, bulletins, and other publications.

Sidran Institute – *www.sidran.org*
Helping people understand, manage, and treat trauma and dissociation.

HELP WITH ADDICTION

Schick Shadel Hospital – *www.schick-shadel.com*
Schick Shadel Hospital has provided alternative alcoholism treatment and a drug rehabilitation since 1935. Its unique medical treatment using counter-conditioning therapy helps patients maintain healthy, productive lifestyles, free of the craving for alcohol or drugs.

Alcoholics Anonymous
www.alcoholics-anonymous.org

Alanon/Alateen
www.alanon.org

BOOKS

Aron, Dr, Elaine. *The Highly Sensitive Person: How to Thrive When the World Overwhelms You*, Broadway Books, 1996

Balch, Phyllis A. and James F. Balch. *Prescription for Nutritional Healing*, Avery Publishing Group, 1997

Bradshaw, John. *Homecoming*, Bantam Books, 1992; *Bradshaw On: The Family*, Health Communications, Inc. 1988

Britten, Rhonda. *Fearless Living*, Penguin Group, 2001

Chopra, Deepak. *Boundless Energy*, Harmony Books, 1995; *Creative Affluence, The A to Z Steps to a Richer Life*, Amber-Allen, 1993

Cohen, Alan. *Dare To Be Yourself*, Fawcett Columbine, 1991

Day, Laura. *Practical Intuition*, Harper Collins, 1997

Forward, Dr. Susan. *Toxic Parents: Overcoming Their Hurtful Legacy and Reclaiming Your Life*, Bantam Books, 1989

Goleman, Daniel. *Emotional Intelligence*, Bantam Books, 1995

Golomb, Dr. Elan. *Trapped In The Mirror: Adult Children of Narcissists and Their Struggle For Self*, Quill William Morris, 1992

Glickstein, Lee. *Be Heard Now*, Broadway Books, 1998

Gray, John. *What You Can Feel You Can Heal; A Guide to Enriching Relationships*, Heart Publishing, 1994; *Men are From Mars Women Are From Venus*, Harper Collins, 1992

Grook, William G. *Chronic Fatigue Syndrome and The Yeast Connection*, Professional Books, 1995

Hanh, Thich Nhat. *Anger: Wisdom For Cooling the Flames*, Riverhead Books, 2001

Hay, Louise. *You Can Heal Your Life*, Hay House, 1984

Horn, Sam. *Take The Bully By The Horns*, St. Martins Press, 1995

Leonard, Linda Schierse. *The Wounded Woman: Healing the Father Daughter Relationship*, Shambala, 1982

McGraw, Dr. Phil. *Self Matters*, Simon & Schuster, 2001

Miller, Alice. *Drama of the Gifted Child: The Search for the True Self*, Basic Books, 1997

Peck, M. Scott. *The Road Less Traveled,* Touchstone Simon & Schuster, 1978

Phillips, Bill. *Body For Life*, Harper Collins 1999

Podell, Ronald M. and Porter Schimer, *Contagious Emotions: Staying Well When Your Loved One is Depressed*, Atria, 1992

Ponder, Catherine. *The Dynamic Laws of Prosperity*, DeVorrs, 1962; *The Dynamic Laws of Healing*, DeVorrs, 1966

Ruiz, Michael. *The Four Agreements*, Amber-Allen Publishing, 1997; *The Mastery of Love*, Amber-Allen Publishing, 1999

Schlessinger, Dr. Laura. *Ten Stupid Things Women Do To Mess Up Their Lives*, Harper Perrenial, 1995

Shinn, Florence Scovel. *The Writings of Florence Scovel Shinn: The Game of Life and How to Play It, Your Word Is Your Wand, The Secret Door to Success, The Power of the Spoken Word*, DeVorrs, 1988

Warren, Neil Clark. *Make Anger Your Ally*, Focus on the Family Publishing, 1990

Zukav, Gary. *The Seat of The Soul*, Fireside Simon & Schuster, 1989

MIND, BODY and SPIRIT

Speaking Circles International
The Art of Full Presence Communication
www.speakingcircles.com
LA Area Facilitator: Lynne Velling
Velling Communication Training
lvelling@vellingcommunicationtraining.com

Toastmasters International
Making Effective Communication a Worldwide Reality
www.toastmasters.org

Body For Life - Bill Phillips
Health, Fitness and Nutritional Help
www.bodyforlife.com/index.asp

Fearless Living Institute
Live Your Life As Your Soul Intended
www.fearlessliving.org

Transpersonal Consultation Group
The Work of Dr. Ron Scolastico
www.ronscolastico.com

Marianne Williamson
The Miracle Matrix
marianne.iamplify.com/home.jsp

Artwork Plates

To Contact The Author

Please visit:
www.alysonkay.com
to view artwork gallery and get updates on
additional resources as they become available.

Look for Alyson Kay's New Books:
Seven Ways to Silence Your Inner Critic
and
The Self Loathers Guide to Greater Self Love
available soon.